AC/DC

In the two years since it was first produced, AC/DC has already acquired a near-legendary status. It has been variously described as 'likely to be seminal to the 70s', 'the first play of the twenty-first century' and 'the kind of work that may save the theatre from being abandoned by the young'. It won Heathcote Williams an Evening Standard drama award in 1970 and the George Devine Award the same year and its extraordinary and electrifying content, form and language have won it acclamation from critics and audiences everywhere.

The play breaks new ground in its exploration of the interlocking psychic vibrations of a group of 'heads', only one of whom is genuine, the rest, in a sense, sparking off him: it is about the pervasive effects of technology and the media and the ways in which certain people try to hit back at them. It is an attack on what the author calls 'psychic capitalism', where the media impose their own fascistic standards on people, instead of being used in a democratic way to provide full information. The author rebels against a stratified concept of characterisation and he shows millions of things batting around in his characters' heads as they attempt communication with each other, against a background of 'group mind', the unnamed and unarticulated contracts that exist between human beings in dialogue. As a result, he has evolved an almost totally new language, which is based not only on his feelings about the media but his very considerable technical knowledge and empathy with his characters.

The play was first produced at The Royal Court Theatre in May 1970, by Nicholas Wright, and has since been revived there twice, in October 1970 as part of the Come Together Festival and in October 1971. It was also produced at The Chelsea Theatre Centre, Brooklyn, New York in 1971.

Heathcote Williams was born in Cheshire in 1941 and before AC/DC wrote a much-praised book about the orators at Speakers' Corner, Hyde Park, entitled The Speakers (1964) and a short play The Local Stigmatic (1967). He is an associate editor of Transatlantic Review.

By the same author:

PLAYSCRIPT 63

AC/DC

Heathcote Williams

JOHN CALDER · LONDON
RIVERRUN PRESS · NEW YORK

First published in Great Britain 1971
by *Gambit*
18 Brewer Street, London W1

First published in this edition 1972
by Calder and Boyars Ltd

Reprinted in this edition 1982 in Great Britain by
John Calder (Publishers) Ltd.,
18 Brewer Street,
London W1R 4AS

And first published in the USA 1983 by
Riverrun Press Inc.,
175 Fifth Avenue,
New York, NY 10010

All performing rights in the play are strictly reserved and applications for performances should be made to
ACTAC Ltd
16 Cadogan Lane, London SW1

No performance of this play may be given unless a licence has been obtained prior to rehearsal

SUBSIDISED BY THE
Arts Council
OF GREAT BRITAIN

Printed in the Channel Islands by The Guernsey Press Co. Ltd.

AC/DC

DRAMA DEPARTMENT
QUEEN MARGARET UNIVERSITY COLLEGE
GATEWAY THEATRE
ELM ROW
EDINBURGH
EH7 4AH

AC/DC was first performed in The Theatre Upstairs at The Royal Court Theatre, London, on May 14th, 1970, with the following cast:

GARY	Robert Lloyd
MELODY	Patricia Quinn
SADIE	Pat Hartley
MAURICE	Henry Woolf
PEROWNE	Ian Hogg

The play was directed by Nicholas Wright.

AC/DC was subsequently presented at The Chelsea Theatre Centre, Brooklyn, New York, by Robert Kalfin and Michael David on February 16th, 1971, with the following cast:

GARY	James Cromwell
MELODY	Jillian Lundig
SADIE	Susan Batson
MAURICE	Ed Zang
PEROWNE	Stefan Gierasch

The play was directed by John Hirsch.

The text of AC/DC is convertible at all points to the frequencies of the actors and the director.

ALTERNATING CURRENT

It is 5 a.m., in an Amusement Arcade. Three people are playing the machines: MOONSHOT, MAGIC CITY, WAYWARD SKULL, TEACHER'S PET, TV BASEBALL, BUCKAROO, and BEAT TIME. Ultra violet lights flashing. The ball bearings churn and wheep through the bumpers, and the neon gates in an electron spin.

BLACK. Three Americans are inside the PHOTOMATON half dressed, with the curtain drawn. The flashlight inside the machine is exploding. From the PHOTOMATON come sounds of heavy breathing, then a symphony of panting, laughing, sucking, billing, and cooing. The rest of the Arcade is in darkness. Flashlights explode in the PHOTOMATON lighting it up from the inside.

GARY. MONGOLIAN CLUSTER FUCK!

MELODY. YEAAAAH! KICKED OUT ALL THE PHYSICAL JAMS!

GARY. GLUED US ALL TOGETHER!

SADIE. *THREE IN ONE AND ONE IN THREE!*

(Laughing and panting they collapse to the floor of the PHOTOMATON, bare legs, and clothes sticking our from under the curtain)

SADIE. *I wanta go solo.*

GARY. Whaaat?

SADIE. *I wanta go solo.*

GARY. We just Blew ourselves together didn't we? We just melted ourselves altogether in a giant gentle atom bomb of sperm and cunt juice, an now she says she wants to go solo . . .

7

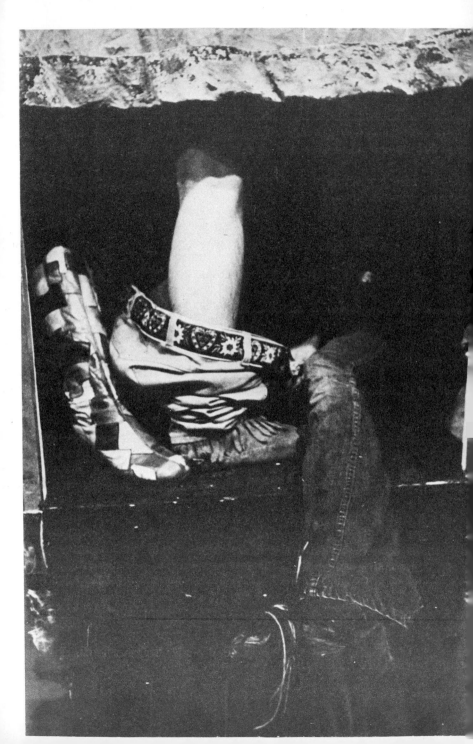

MELODY. Chinese Portraits. Come on. That'll zip us up. That'll get us together. That'll give us a real deep interbrain buzz. Ok Sadie?

SADIE. Ok.

MELODY. Come on now, I'm holding someone really tight in my head. I'm right into someone now!

GARY. OK...OK. What kinda... (Sound of snapping fingers) What kinda restaurant he or she remind you of?

MELODY. Hot dog kennel.

GARY. Ha!

SADIE. What kinda wallpaper . . . he or she remind you of?

MELODY. Oriental grass.

GARY. Shit, I'm gonna burn if its me.

MELODY. YEAH, We'll wash your ego right out!

GARY. What kinda colour?

MELODY. We had that before, last time we played.

GARY. Who for?

MELODY. Dunno. But whoever it was they gotta high evaporation rate!

GARY. Ha.

SADIE. What kinda flavour?

MELODY. All snarled up. Like anchovies . . .

GARY. It's Sadie! Its Sadie.

MELODY. Yeah! Right! (Flashbulb explodes) Cooled you out Sadie!

SADIE. *Yeah. Ha.*

GARY. O.K. O.K. Come on now, I'm holding someone really tight now.

MELODY. Ok er . . . What kinda . . . What kinda musical instrument?

GARY. Mouthorgan.

MELODY. It's himself. He's chosen himself!

GARY. No. No its not.

SADIE. *What kinda dirty habit?*

GARY. Leaving the toilet unflushed.

MELODY. I wouldn't leave the toilet unflushed for fear of your robbing it.

SADIE. *What kinda food?*

GARY. A long white crisp cos lettuce.

SADIE. *What kinda scent?*

GARY. Testosterone.

SADIE. *It's Melody!*

GARY. Right.

MELODY. Me? What's testosterone got to do with me? You're switching everyone round.

GARY. That's right! It's a good way to stay fresh.

MELODY. Ha! Yeah!

SADIE. *Kicked out all the flesh jams! Kicked out all the psychic jams.*

GARY. Glued us all together.

MELODY. The Synergetic Conspiracy!

SADIE. *Stereochemical Egodectomy!*

(GARY and MELODY draw aside the curtain, and file out of the PHOTOMATON, pulling their clothes back on. Full lights)

GARY. Wow! (Stretching) Everybody's crash landed right into the middle of everyone else's fuckin buzz, right?

MELODY. Up into the air, Junior Birdmen! Hey, where are you man?

(GARY holds his hand about two foot above his head)

MELODY. Right! Healed all the crimps. Hey, we really laid some changes on each other, no? I feel completely Burst, completely Deconditioned. Just like I been doing some astral projections and I just slipped back into my body this second and its a Perfect Fit.

GARY. Yeah! I knew a man once who didn't get back in time and his body didn't fit. (He makes a series of paralysed movements)

MELODY. Ha! (Touching him) Wow! Triple Interbrain BUZZZZZZ (Drawing her breath through her teeth) Flushed all our aliases down that iron lung. (She points to the PHOTOMATON, and then goes back to it, and takes out the photo strips from the delivery bay of the machine)

GARY. Transferred every one's evil ego vibes, yeah! Transferred them into the photos. Free floating. (Flapping his arms)

MELODY. Yeah! (She folds up the photostrips and tears them up, and then slides them up and down against each other, so that all their features are mixed up)

GARY. Wow! (Looking closely over MELODY's shoulder) Wow!

MELODY. Hey, look at this. Your nose, see, my eyes. Your tits, my eyes, Sadie's cunt. Ha! Triple Interbrain Buzzzzzz!

GARY. Hey, SADIE! Come on out and dig this!

SADIE. *(from inside the PHOTOMATON) There's another little buzz I wanta get out of this machine and then we can get really spaced.*

GARY. Ha.

MELODY. Oh come on, I'm spaced out already (To herself, staring at the photos) So many days left unstoned.

SADIE. *(from inside, flashing the flashbulbs) Turn on satellite control, start ampex recorder. Computer to run condition. Computer print-out reading all zeros. Activate sun gun and direct light beam at Sun sensor. Sun pulse indication appearing on computer print-out . . . Check raster scan . . .*

GARY. Come on out, Sadie.

MELODY. Yeah, you're givin us the space dumps.

GARY. (pointing to the PHOTOMATON) It's not a space capsule, its an iron lung!

(MELODY giggles)

SADIE. *De-activate Sun Gun. Main battery deep discharge. Chamber bleed up. Pre shipment Comprehensive. Main battery deep discharge. PRE-SHIPMENT BUTTON UP! VROOOOOM! WE HAVE LIFT OFF!*

MELODY. (sticking her neck out, and shouting at SADIE in the machine) They don't allow women to work in the Space Programme, didn't you know? The acidity of their skin, once a month, it interferes with the delicate components.

GARY. You'll have to stick to Inner Space, baby.

SADIE. *(from inside the machine) Inner Space is over-populated.*

MELODY. (turning away, and looking at the photostrips. To GARY) Hey, you know I should have my photograph taken every five minutes all my life, then I could flick through the photographs and watch myself grow older. Hey, look at that one! I was doing that one twenty different ways in my head, and look how its come out.

GARY. Yeah. Marlon Brando was in the paper the other day, you know, and he was complaining to a Finnish photographer that photographers were always photographing him with a transitional expression on his face.

MELODY. Yeah?

SADIE. *(quietly) Media freaks.*

(MAURICE, dressed in a white coat, has been bent over the machine WEST CLUB, repairing it. The backboard of the machine has been stripped off, baring thick skeins of wires and valves. He moves across to GARY and MELODY, standing behind them as they examine their photos)

MAURICE. I used to work as a sound engineer on Henry Hall's Guest Night before I came here. I was responsible for blowing up all people like that to double their size so that they couldn't invite me. They were just started off as a pilot signal, only Perowne made me turn the volume up so they're coming through now as a permanent fuckin echo. He's stuffed Marlon Brando in me kartso (Pointing to his crotch), he's stuffed Jayne Mansfield in me cunt, and Lee Marvin in me liver finger, and pushing Mia Farrow's babies through me nipples; and he's got the rods and cones in my eyes as Radio receivers and Transmitters to a very first hand frequency so that the way that that fuckin outfit exploits my photoconductivity can't never stop . . .

MELODY. Wow!

GARY. HEY, SADIE! DIG THIS!

MELODY. YEAH, HE'S REALLY SPACED! See if you can hit HIS Buzz with your space-craft.

(SADIE emerges from the PHOTOMATON. She stares at MAURICE, then turns to MELODY)

SADIE. Oh come on, stop laying all that second-hand head talk on everyone you meet.

MAURICE. (to GARY) I don't mind Lee Marvin getting a charge off me, but when I get it back from him, its the wrong fuckin amperage.

GARY. That's right. Huh, that's Right!

MELODY. (to GARY) Hey, stay loose, stay loose.

MAURICE. (moving in on GARY) Perowne filled my teeth in a certain way, you see, certain alloys in certain combinations, so that I was picking up tv programmes in my head like a Jew's Harp, and he shoved David Niven-Richard-Harris-Hemmings-Photo-down my arteries and dialling my head very hard, and switching my body clock on, off, on, off, and every time I kissed Perowne I was forced to desalivate because of course Perowne didn't want David Niven's style of kissing, and After I'd kissed Perowne I had to Defecate, i.e. make myself not Feke any more, and if I didn't Defecate after, they'd file down the David-Niven-Pat Boone-fuckin-Hemming-Head to a Sharp Point and when it'd made its transmissions from my fuckin eye, it'd whip round and down to my optic nerve and SLASH IT TO BITS ...

GARY. Hey! All the People he's into!

MELODY. (nudging him) Yeah ... Hey! Remember Sadie on that trip?

GARY. What? Oh Wow, all those telegrams. (To MAURICE) Yeah, She was on a trip like that. She was sending telegrams to all those people. Who was it? David Niven?

SADIE. No, (laughs) it was J. Paul Getty.

GARY. Oh, yeah, J. Paul Getty. Ha. Yeah (To MAURICE) Sadie picks up on him sitting in his black leather swivel chair, combing his hair with his check stubs, right? and he wires Sadie. "Thank you Sadie for wasting this groovy idea about me combing my hair with checkstubs, but I am not rich, I cannot sign a check for five cents. I'll tell you my secret. I am meagrely paid by a Syndicate of the rich to be the Public Rich Man and the Easy Target Decoy. I am doing you a favour telling you this. Tell no one. Love Paul."

MELODY. (to MAURICE) It's an E.S.P. telegram. Sent collect. You dig? So Sadie gets out her scratch-pad: "Dear Paul, thanks for the memo anent your position. I sympathise with your position, because I am paid by a Syndicate of the FAMOUS to be the Public Famous Person, as a decoy, to preserve their Anonymity. Love to your bald head, Signed Sadie."

GARY. Ha! that was groovy.

SADIE. *(to MAURICE distantly) Who's Perowne?*

MAURICE. Who's Perowne? Perowne has me washing my hands every hour, the other day, because he said they weren't any good any more as exTENsores you see, and I should try and wear them away. Friend of mine, Colney Hatch, said there was a whole mob at that already and if I wanted to get that through, I'd have to top it up a bit, i.e. cut them off at the joints (laying his finger across his wrist)

(SADIE laughs. GARY and MELODY move closer to MAURICE, pointing at him)

MELODY. Scatter language!

GARY. Yeah, and Metonymic Distortion.

MELODY. Synaesthetic Conglomerates!

GARY. Interpenetration of Themes. Neologisms!

MELODY. Twelve tone dirty jokes.

GARY. Delaminated word salad!

MELODY. The Asyndetic Putsch!

GARY. When are they going ta release the flip side of your speech center? We could do some great sleeve notes.

MELODY. (slowly, staring at MAURICE) Do you know what a schizoid metonym is Maurice? When the first man said: The Kettle is Boiling, it was noted down as a schizoid metonym by those present, because, as everyone knows, its not the kettle but the water that boils. But, as the first man to say this phrase, quietly struggled in his straitjacket, his chroniclers, his gazeteers, and his warders, who were taking tea at the time, conversed amiably: "The Kettle is Boiling, the Kettle is Boiling, the kettle is boiling . . ." congratulating themselves on the economy of their language. So, keep on with it, some of it'll get through the customs.

GARY. (to MELODY) Except there may be EVEN MORE economic linguistic structures around . . . than the one he's using.

MELODY. Yeah? You're puttin me on.

GARY. No, there's a language called Mescalero in which none of the verbs are tensed.

MELODY. So?

GARY. Well, none of the verbs in that language have any TIME sense. You dig? (closing up to MELODY, cuddling her) Maybe we ought to learn that language. People who speak that language probably LIVE longer.

MELODY. Ha!

SADIE. (staring) Have you just gone into Public Relations?

GARY. No, why? Do you wanna join in my private life?

SADIE. What are you trying to whittle away at his trip for?

MAURICE. (waving at SADIE) That's all right, that's all right. (To GARY and MELODY) LOOOOOK, I got triple realities going on in slip language the whole fuckin time, but I can get my Influencing Machine talking Cool Straight Police Car Language from the

Clapham Toilet Bureau, any day of the week, when there's someone who can ONLY BE NAILED like that. (Speaking in an American accent, and gesticulating in ham, servile gestures) NOW, EXCUSE ME MADAM, WHERE CAN I CLOSET FOR YOU YOUR COAT? Get it? I'm not joining your private life because I've been told to keep out of my own. And as to what you said earlier: fuckin schizoid metonym. I'll go into that very deeply (Tugging at MELODY, dragging her down to the ground) Loook, what have I got here? Look, this is my sock. Do you know what I've got in my sock? (Sitting on the ground, he feels a swelling in his sock, and pulls it down) I've got chocolate tinfoil, with tenebrations five point eight, I've got crucified orange peel, with tenebrations six point ten, I've got butterfly excrement with tenebrations eight point nine, and my whole sock's painted with British Museum Leather Dressing Solution. AND WHAT DO YOU THINK I KEEP ALL THIS SHIT IN THERE FOR? TO WARD OFF FUCKIN SCHIZO-PHRENICS!

SADIE. *(roaring with laughter) Right on! Right on!*

GARY. (to SADIE) You wanta pick up on That?

SADIE. *Yeah, that cat's a real high energy dude!*

MELODY. (getting up) He's really thick with being a schizo.

MAURICE. RIGHT! (Pulling at his scalp) And this is where three phrenologists lost their fingernails. In me riah. In me fuckin barnet. And five years ago, they shaved it all off, pasted wires on, and plugged me into their so-called amnesiac shockers. But I broke the box, and fused every light in the area for thirty miles.

SADIE. *RIGHT ON! (SADIE laughs, grabs hold of MAURICE, they growl at each other, and then roll over each other on the floor grappling, and laughing)*

GARY. (pointing at them) Hey, that was a quick seduction. You pinched her sloshy boobs. You chewed her bee stung lips . . .

MELODY. (standing over them shouting) You scarfed her box out, then you let her go down on you, and give you head, in spite of her awful ortho-creme mouthwash, then you shoved your raunchy little dick up her butt, sawed her to bits, with your toad testicles screech-ing to a halt, and she had an abortion . . .

GARY. (shouting) An you drilled her again. Ya got married. Ya separated . . .

MELODY. An she got custody of the kids. (At MAURICE) Hey Schizo! you really moved it.

GARY. Yeah! Advertise your fantasies widely enough an you're bound to get Someone to populate them.

MELODY. Acid Positive!

(MAURICE and SADIE collapse breathless underneath the PHOTOMATON. GARY and MELODY move across to one of the pinmachines BEAT TIME. SADIE looks up and watches a man standing beside the machine that is being repaired: WEST CLUB. Its glass cover is off. He is picking the ball bearings out of the sump, and rolling them with his hands against the inside edges of the pin-table)

SADIE. Is that Perowne?

MAURICE. Yes. He's been trying to go bald a lot, but there's always one hair holds the others up.

(PEROWNE breaks off momentarily, and stands clasping his hands together, cracking the joints, then holding them tightly together)

SADIE. Why's he holding his hands like that?

MAURICE. So that only one of his hands need do the sweating. He's getting a displacement current going, because there's a Dead Field Structure moving round those (Pointing at GARY and MELODY), and I've been building up his resistance to that Dead Field. I've got him up to 25 megohms already.

(PEROWNE leans over the slotmachine, staring at it)

PEROWNE. A ball is cued from a corner on an N times M foot table, at an angle of forty five degrees (N and M are integers). How many sides will the ball strike before it again goes into the corner? (Drawing a pencil across the glass) You tesselate the first quadrant with M time N rectangles. By reflection each boundary intersected by the line X equals Y, corresponds to a side struck by a ball cued from the origin at a forty five degree angle. The line X equals Y first intersects a vertex at (L,L) where L is the lowest common multiple of M, N and en route intersects L/N-1 vertical and L/M-1 horizontal boundaries. Accordingly, the ball strikes L/N-1 + L/M-2 =(M+N) L/MN-2 sides. The result may also be stated (M+N) (M,N) - 2, where (,) indicates the greatest common divisor. (Looking up—moving away from the machine) Five and a half hours ago, I was in Imperial College Library, and I discovered that the problem had already been set in the Pi Mu Epsilon Journal of Mathematics in 1959, and solved by the following people: J.G. Abad, J.P. Celenz, Yu Chang, R.B. Eggleston, Michael Goldberg, R.S. Kaluzniacki, R.L. Kammerer, Liselotte Miller, Edward Moylan, Robert Patenande, Stanton Philip, J.M. Quoniam, Steven Ruse, J.J. Segedy, K.N. Sigmon, T.R. Smith, Laurence Somer, Steven Tice, P.S. Vitta, Allan Wache, John Wessner, Oswald Wyler and J.W. Zerger.

SADIE. (Standing up) Yeah. Well, no emotion's worth having twice.

PEROWNE. You know what your lifetime's storage capacity is? Ten to the power of seven bits. That's all. I've wasted four, five, maybe Ten bits on that (Pointing at the pin table). WHY DON'T THEY KEEP THE IMPRINTS CLEAN? The thing was shopsoiled from the Start. Centralised Data Storage. That's all it needs. The simplest thing. Centralised Data Storage.

(PEROWNE moves towards MAURICE and SADIE, holding his hands together. Cracking the fingers. He seems armoured. Totally encased)

MAURICE. (getting up) You've been over-amping.

PEROWNE. (stares at him. Smiles quietly at him, then recognises him) Hello. (clasps him looking at SADIE) Hello.

MAURICE. What else you been going?

(PEROWNE stares at him, clasps his hands again, and twists his head tensely)

SADIE. *(loudly) What made you have the emotion in the first place?*

PEROWNE. Do you mean mathematics? I don't know. Its a sentimental metaphor: mathematics. I used to work for IBM as a researcher. They were a lot of superstitious mafiosos. (Twisting his head) I'm trying to get through to something on my own.

SADIE. *Einstein was psychotic.*

PEROWNE. I just watched a programme about Einstein. Einstein apparently said that to explain soup was probably not the same as tasting it. If he was so uneasy about it, why did he choose such a boring example?

There might be a thought somewhere about Einstein starting to SCREAM at the taste of soup. (PEROWNE starts twisting again, and looks at MAURICE) I've been watching a lot of television.

MAURICE. You've got fuckin radiated, haven't you? You've got fuckin media rash haven't you?

PEROWNE. (moving closer to him) I feel a little over-loaded. (Smiles weakly at him)

MAURICE. What else you been doing?

PEROWNE. Well, I watched the news. The television. You see. I watched the news (twitching) Then I went into the street.

Whole place is a noisy ashtray. Then ... Then I met a boy from the ... London Street Commune. I listened to every word he said ... I even suggested they take over a whole street. Knock the connecting walls of the houses together, build a refectory table on the ground floor, and a refectory bed on the top floor running the whole length of the street. I enjoyed talking to him. But it was too ... he gave me a ... I ... I had to Drink Him Off ... I got ... double-exPOSED. I ... Some kind of sensory Bottleneck ... I feel a bit ... double exposed. He Bared His Teeth A Lot ... it was ...

MAURICE. (holding him) You got overloaded haven't you.

PEROWNE. YES (Moving his shoulder inside his clothes) YES.

MAURICE. (springing away) RIGHT! I can clear all those tracks. The Boy with the Heady Views ... The Mathematics ... The Drink Track ... The TV News programme I can flash all those tracks clean as a whistle for you again.

PEROWNE. (staring at him, smiles) You can?

MAURICE. (Placing his hands on PEROWNE's head, gripping tufts of hair, moving PEROWNE's scalp across his skull. Closing his eyes) Can I? I'm pitching into the boy you met with the heady views right now. I've got to get the exact Anti-Dotal Wave Form you see. To rub off that track for you. I've Got It! I've Got it! (closing his eyes, rocking his head) I'm getting an engram of Exact Weight to discharge you. I've got it! I've got it! What this (Screwing up his face, eyes closed)? I'm going to the airport to meet them? From Barcelona: Oswald Mosley, and William Joyce with their twisted tuning fork (Drawing a swastika in the air) and from Glasgow: Palme Dutt and Harry Pollitt with their tin opener (Draws a hammer and sickle in the air) What's happening? What's happening? They won't let them through the customs. They're making them take a urine test. They're looking for the pink spot in the urine that's going round now as fashionable. One of them said he had had it, but he'd wasted it. Another one started chucking all papers into the air. He said somebody'd bought it off him before he could go into it. Only one of them refused to take it: I'm leakin nothing, he said. A slip of the lip costs a ship. Huh. None of them are getting it. They've got to take the first plane back. They're letting them keep their samples though. The glass pipettes.

(PEROWNE laughs. MAURICE bends down over PEROWNE and touches heads)

A Clean Break? I hit it?

PEROWNE. (smiling) Pretty much. (He begins to move in a less armoured way)

MAURICE. I switched you fit of that track right?

PEROWNE. Yes.

SADIE. Why do you have to put it into words?

MAURICE. I KNOW. I KNOW. Every word that I utter is the radioactive waste of eighteen million telepathons. Every word that's pumped through me is eighteen million telepathons down the drain. I don't Want to use words.

SADIE. Why doncha use karate sound blows on him, to clear all his hangups? (To PEROWNE) You know about that? Practitioners place a rat at a hundred yards distant from their mouth, then pitch into the rat's frequency, sound off, and the rat drops dead. Sonic laser beams.

PEROWNE. What does it sound like?

SADIE. KIIIIIIIIIIIYAAAAAAAAAAAAAAAAAAAAAA!

PEROWNE. KIIIIIIIIIIIIIIIIIYYYYYYYYAAAAAAAAAAAAAAAAAAAAA AAAAAAHH!!

(GARY and MELODY emerge from the other part of the Arcade)

GARY. What's going on now?

MAURICE. **What's going on between Perowne and me is peak to peak amplitude.**

GARY. Yeah? Well you wave your length, and I'll wave mine.

(MELODY laughs)

SADIE. *Oh shutup, they're behind some heavy shit.*

MELODY. Yeah? (Looking at PEROWNE) Hey, he looks wired up.

GARY. He's gone solo years back.

MELODY. He was twitching all the time.

GARY. He was really chewin out some inner riff.

MELODY. (to PEROWNE) Why were you twitching?

PEROWNE. I've been watching television. Television always makes me twitch.

MELODY. We'll cool you out. See that Photomaton? We just turned that into an orgone chamber. We had a Mongolian Cluster Fuck in there just now. Get in there and pick up the vibes we left in there. That'll cool you right out.

MAURICE. **Leave him alone (Holding PEROWNE) I'm the only one that can get into his head and clear the tracks. I'm picking up his brain waves and picking up his alpha rhythms . . . I know exactly which tracks got blocked.**

PEROWNE. (staring at him, smiling) Yes.

MAURICE. **Right. Ha. I'll take the . . . (flipping his fingers,** pointing at the bottle) I'll take the drink as a starter. 1961. 1961 being pumped through now Perowne. Ha. (Leaning forward) I'm in a clinic in the Dordogne, France. I find out the S.P. They're short on alcoholics. So, two days later, to extend my visa, I have them find me scammered in a ditch with eight bottles of Pernod. They bring me back, fill me up with Brands Essence and a raw egg, lay me flat. Now this place is run by a shrink and his lady who wrote some very famous books in the thirties about her previous life as the Queen of Egypt.

PEROWNE. I've heard of her.

MAURICE. And their method of cure, Perowne, is Regressive Hypnotism. They start the cure. She's on call all the time to see that I don't turn out to have been anyone more famous than her, in a previous reincarnation. How old are you, Maurice? 23. Right, he says, lie down on the bed, take off your shoes, and stare at that stud in ceiling. Like all hypnotists, he's got ophthalmic goitre, and he keeps the stud in the ceiling as a . . .

PEROWNE. An understudy.

MAURICE. Relax your right leg. Move your right leg. You can't move your right leg? Right, we're off. Now, Maurice, I'm going to count from 23 to 1, and when I get to one you will lose touch with my physical voice. He counts me back down my ages . . . 23, 22, 21 . . . and every number he calls out, I'm to remember things . . . 13, 12, 11 . . . little things coming out every number. Then his voice gets fainter; we get to 2, then 1. I still remember things: nappy rash, gripe water, cock like a snail just been given a prussic acid dip. Then, Zero. Nothing. Minus One. Nothing. I remember nothing. Minus 2. I can't come up with a thing. His voice is fainter and fainter. Minus Three. Nothing. Then, very low: Minus Four, Maurice . . . And then I'M SHOUTING, PEROWNE, AND I'M FLAILING ABOUT ON THE BED, AND I'M JERKING ABOUT AND I'M ALL OVER THE PLACE AND I'M SHOUTING: THEY'RE CUTTING MY TONGUE, STOP

THEM, STOP THEM, THEY'RE CUTTING MY TONGUE OUT . . . I know he's bringing the Queen of Egypt in from the next room. I can see her face. Its white. They try to count me back up again, but I'm stuck at minus four, my age of minus four: THEY'RE CUTTING MY TONGUE OUT, THEY'RE CUTTING MY TONGUE OUT . . . and he's going minus 4, minus 3, minus 2, minus 1, nothing, 1,2,3,4, . . . 21,22,23. Up and down, up and down SEVEN times to fetch me back, and eventually they do. But I can't speak. I'm just going (mouthing) . . . So they counted me back down again, to minus four, to fetch my tongue off the people, then back to 23. I stood up. Drank three jugs of water straight off, and I said to her: Your face is very white. I am going to do a level-shift, she says, and she covers her eyes. I can see a dark cell, she says, covered with straw, somewhere outside Barcelona. You're a spy. In the Spanish Civil War. You're refusing to pass information. They're cutting your tongue out as a last ditch stand. That is all. Then she comes out of her level-shift, swings her external camera onto me, and says: They cut your tongue out, in that incarnation, and this left a bleeding scar on your supraphysical self and your etheric body, which you have had to assuage by excessive drinking. The Lunar Stagnancy is finished. The waters are no longer violent. (MAURICE takes the bottle off PEROWNE, takes a shot from it, and puts it into his pocket). A clean Break?

PEROWNE. A clean break.

MAURICE. They said they'd never had such results. So, I free loaded there for a couple of weeks, until the word got around they were suddenly going to be short of pernicious catatonics, and I didn't feel like filling that one up for them: ripping off bigger and bigger scabs and eating myself . . . die in ten days; so, I left. I went to Paris. But I was extremely grateful to her for having allowed to have fought the Spanish Civil War, in a previous incarnation.

PEROWNE. Yes. Where did you stay?

MAURICE. I stayed in Hotel d'Alsace. Where Oscar Wilde died. But anyway in the Next Room of this hotel was staying a man called Wittgenstein or Frere, I can't remember which. He was historian. Struck up conversation with him, and you know what he told me? Only the RIGHT side cut people's tongues out in the Spanish Civil War, so that I must have been on the WRONG SIDE

PEROWNE. She'd swindled you. (PEROWNE stares at MAURICE, then reaches for the bottle in MAURICE's pocket. MAURICE moves away)

MAURICE. No. (Staring at PEROWNE, rubbing the bottle in his pocket) Still a faint flicker? isn't there? Still a faint flicker from that drunk track. Right. I'm gonna swab you down completely now. Little microwave welding to switch you fit of that aspect completely. (chanting) Brendan Behan, Dielan Thomas, Churchill-hill, which one do you want? (Closes his eyes)

It's all right now, I'm picking him up.

Huh. I had to dress up in jodhphurs and show him the skid marks on my knickers. (Holding PEROWNE's hair) I caught him creaming his pants once when the local lending library caught fire. He was a lesbian . . .

PEROWNE. It's Dylan Thomas?

MAURICE. (rocking his head trance like) I'm catching Dieland Thomas leaving electro-magnetic patterns of himself outside the Black Horse and Cafe Ann. Anyone standing there now has cranial drunk patterns and changes into him. Their bowels get corrupted to his frequency. I have to get there first to save Perowne from his emissions and depolarise him on that score.

SADIE. Ha.

MAURICE. (to PEROWNE, holding PEROWNE's head in his hands) Flashing Him Through to De-Imprint you, right?

(PEROWNE nods)

MELODY. How the fuck can you de-imprint anyone?

SADIE. *FOLD UP YA FUNKY DISHRAG, that's how.*

MELODY. Ah, CRANK UP YA TONGUE AN KEEP IT INSIDE YA HEAD.

GARY. THINKS HER STINKIN NASTY'S LINED WITH MINK.

SADIE. *LOOK SHIT-HEEL, GET OUTTA MY TRIP, OR I'LL BUST YA PRO-GRAMMED LITTLE NUTS!*

MELODY. Anyone feel de-imprinted?

SADIE. *Yeah! I'm beginning to!*

GARY. (pointing at MAURICE indicating Sadie) Tie her to your tail, she's just the right voltage for all that vintage schizoid shit.

MAURICE. (ignoring them, closing his eyes, and changing his voice: three syllables for the price of one, he speaks in Dylan Thomas's voice, and pours away the bottle of drink at the same time) Dieland Thomas being pumped thro me now to clear up Perowne's drunk tracks. I am no Boily Solitary Lover, Tuning Up his Unnotched nerve, and Crying OH MAN! BE MY SIMILE. I am the Ghost that Goes for Any thing in Sheets! But I shall sell the blind worm in my Thighs down the Old Kent Road.

(Going back into his own voice)

I'm the heir to Shake-speare, he said to me; I said you're the anal heir, no one else's. Get off my back you fuckin Druid tart.

(PEROWNE gets up, smiles, and moves around the

(Slotpalace as if something has been taken off his shoulders, his movements now flowing where they were just now constricted. SADIE looks from MAURICE to PEROWNE intrigued.)

SADIE. I saw Dylan on the subway the other day. He had a green nosebag filled with laughing gas. One more breath and the whole history . . . the whole history of . . . (Almost psyched by the energy flowing between PEROWNE and MAURICE) . . . the whole history of something would have been different.

GARY. Oh man (To PEROWNE) Do you know why women can never deliver good epigrams? Its because of the nature of the orgasm. A man's orgasm is INtensive, right, and a woman's orgasm is EXtensive.

MELODY. Sure is. Ha! Hey, she's talking about Bob Dylan an they're talking about Dylan Thomas. Everyone's Gettin Spread Around! We're getting right back into that Beatiful ego loss that we had going just now in the Photomaton.

GARY. Yeah! (Pointing at MAURICE and PEROWNE) Hey, Let's get Five in One and One in Five!

(PEROWNE disappears into the Photomaton. SADIE wanders off into another part of the Arcade)

MELODY. (pointing at MAURICE) Yeah, let's spread EVERYONE around.

GARY. Get out your scratch pad Melody. Telegram. Museum of Modern Art New York. My name is . . . What's your name troll?

MAURICE. My sister slated it up to hollow me out. She stuck Maurice Chevalier, Maurice Kaufman and Maurice O'Dwyer on her pay roll before she did it.

GARY. (taking the bottle off MAURICE) My name is

Maurice, and I read of your forthcoming kinetic art exhibit. I will stand in front of wall C.2., (I have seen your map come guide in the hallway), and I will drink myself to death in three days. Please give my forthcoming visit full coverage. When the public have seen your exhibit, me, and my kinetic death, they will leave your museum and go out into the street and look at people differently, which is your current squalid gambit. Please give my forthcoming visit full coverage . . .

MAURICE. Looooook! I can get drunk on the smell of lamp-post wine.

MELODY. Know what Joan of Arc said, Maurice? She said, I find if I drink heavily and then blow a loud whistle very hard, the voices go away (Taking the bottle off GARY and handing it to MAURICE) Here, this is what you want isn't it? Go on, its not every day that someone picks you up so good.

MAURICE. For me to say 'it is', that's a prepared game. So, fuck off. (Going closer) Look, these personality techniques you're trying on me, any beatnik would scoff out of court. In fact, that beatnik would go back to his personality of 1946, and say I Don't Like The Cut of Your Jib, My Man, in order to finish you off . . . So, shove.

MELODY. (to GARY) What kinda . . . What kinda . . . destination . . . he or she remind you of?

GARY. Destination?

MELODY. Yeah, like religious destination. Like Sheol, like Hades, yeah? Like Atlantis, Elysium, Valhalla, Gehinnom . . . Kismet.

GARY. (staring at MAURICE) A bar, permanently open, like a running sore.

MAURICE. (shouting) The drinks got nothing to do with me, you silly cunt. I was demagnetising Perowne.

MELODY. Demagnetising? Whatcha mean demagnetising?

MAURICE. All right. I'll put it very simply for you. I was being Perowne's Jesuit Confessor just then if you like. He said to me: The Divinity behaved hysterically at three points in HUMAN time: his birth, the marriage feast, and his death. I put my hand through the grille, I warmed up his balls, and I said: Never mind, father, the upper classes still call their dogs by working class names.

MELODY. I don't understand.

GARY. Insane (To MELODY) Who's PEROWNE anyway?

MELODY. YEAH! I mean there's so much fuckin static in here you don't know Who's Who, do you?

(PEROWNE puts his head through the cutain of the PHOTOMATON)

PEROWNE. I can see what you're trying to do. Spreading everyone around. It's entirely unnecessary. Spreading Maurice around anyway (Coming out) Maurice was in court the other day, and they asked him to give his name, and he said his name was Dead Wood pronounced East Light. There were several people present who could see that he was going to be asked Why, and prepared the appropriate expressions on their faces. Maurice said: Because my stomach thinks your throat is cut.

(SADIE emerges laughing from the back of the Arcade)

MELODY. (pointing at her) And I wouldn't suck you with HER mouth.

GARY. Aaaaah ha ha ... (Moving towards PEROWNE) We can spread YOU around though, can't we?

MELODY. Right

GARY. (studying PEROWNE) What kinda . . . sex, he or she remind you of??

MELODY. A wink-off. Takes two years.

GARY. Ha. And?

MELODY. Mmmn . . . Goosing people with records of Winston Churchill wartime speeches.

GARY. And?

MELODY. Fellatio. In the mouth of an alcoholic.

GARY. The Wrong Substance for the Wrong Appetite!

MELODY. (twitching, in imitation of PEROWNE) It's not Ergonomic!

GARY. Perowne?

MELODY. Perowne.

PEROWNE. What are you doing here?

GARY. WE'RE COSMIC SHIT AND HER SPASM BAND!

(They move around PEROWNE snapping their fingers)

PEROWNE. Do you play Music?

GARY. MUSIC? You know where Music is on the electromagnetic spectrum? It's down there, by your feet. No, man, we just get up on the stage an send out vibrations. Silent Vibrations.

MELODY. We send out silent mantras and mudras that Kill people. We pick up on the audience. We steal all

THEIR vibrations, then we mess them all together and we give them back to them Minus their egos.

PEROWNE. Where do you play?

GARY. Where? We gotta coupla gigs.

SADIE. *We don't play anywhere. If we're sending out vibrations, people will pick them up wherever they are. We don't need any Stage for them to pick up on it. We don't need any of that Media shit.*

(PEROWNE smiles)

MELODY. We need a stage.

SADIE. *Uhuh? well drop down an get on it.*

MAURICE. (To GARY and MELODY) Perowne is a very complicated person. You can't catch up with him. With your tatty Chinese Portraits. He's So secretive that one of these days he's going to disappear up his own arsehole. He's a psycholinguist. He can kill off hundreds of years of your lives with one joke, and so can I. I'm his agent.

MELODY. (to PEROWNE) What's you psychic colour?

MAURICE. Whatever you say his psychic colour is, he's having it dyed.

(PEROWNE sits down, takes hold of SADIE's suitcase, and puts it on his lap. Then he goes through it, fondling a pink shirt inside it. He gradually pulls it out of the case, and slowly furls it around his head, pulling it tighter and tighter.)

GARY. (pointing at PEROWNE) Hey, look at the soles of his shoes. Wow. Look at them. Not a scratch see. Not a scratch on them.

MELODY. Yeah. He must lead a soft life.

GARY. Maybe his feet never touch the ground.

SADIE. *Oh what are you pokin up all these negative vibes for?*

MELODY. So that we can all take off again.

(GARY notices PEROWNE twisting the shirt tighter and tighter around his head)

GARY. (to MAURICE) You sure you demagnetised him, huh? Because I'm still picking up a bit of karmic congestion there.

MAURICE. You are. And that's because of the TV programme he was listening to. I've got to burn off that track right now. (To SADIE) Fuckin Newsreader leaving his live cigarette ends in Perowne's stomach 9.30. (To PEROWNE) What was one of the programmes about?

PEROWNE. (turning, then twisting the shirt tighter and tighter, and pulling at his head) Nepal . . . something . . . NEPAL.

(MAURICE darts around the Slotpalace, touching and pointing to the Slotmachines)

MAURICE. Autocue . . . Master Switch . . . Soundboom . . . Videophones . . . Flick flick . . . hello, this one's leaking sixty cycles a second to help us out. (He stands behind the machine WEST CLUB, behind the raised glass of the broken machine, as if on TV) Flick flick.

(He splays his hands, and waves them horizontally in front of his face. SADIE goes over and stands in front of the screen, and near PEROWNE's chair. She meshes her fingers in front of MAURICE's face, and vibrates them. She splays her hands and moves them quickly against each other, creating an optical illusion of flicker.)

SADIE. STROBE STROBE FROM THE MONITOR SCREEN! LINE BEAT THE LINE BEATER! (Moving her hands faster) PSYCHIC TEEVEE STUDIOS!

MAURICE. I want it up to the critical flicker frequency (Pointing at SADIE's hands, MAURICE speaks through the glass, only the top half of his body visible. Mechanical chant) ITV Newsroom 9.30 Caught you hollowing out Perowne's Travel Instincts and Striped Muscle Responses in a Cheap Fuckin Way. Bio-Photo-Metric reduction of Perowne 70 grams. Reduction of Perowne's capacitance, 17 microfarads. (To SADIE) FASTER FASTER. These are the details omitted . . .

SADIE. These are THE DETAILS OMITTED, NEWSBUG!

GARY. Hey hey hey.

MELODY. (laughing) He's really groovin on Sadie's head now. Remember the time Sadie was so tripped out on Marshall McLuhan she sprayed the tv with communion wine an licked her way through the screen?

MAURICE. (shouting in a high chant, vibrating his hands, creating flicker effect) FASTER! FASTER! These are the details omitted: In Nepal, CUNT, they believe in Sympathetic Magic, and when a woman is late in giving birth or a Cow in Calving, they rub their bellies with RAILWAY tickets, as Railway Engines are the fastest things they know. SO, NEWSREADER CUNT, has my request for a Grip Bag filled with Concorde Jet Plane tickets been televised? So that I can deliver Perowne from all your pranky tenebrations at Top Speed? NO. I know who is dealing with this, and I also laughed at it, until I realised that it was childishly seducing. In any case, the electrical "e" was taken out of my name to Run the Concorde so you'd have only been doubling up . . .

SADIE. We're Squashing you, Newsbug!

MELODY. (to GARY) Hey, Sadie's gettin really leechy.

Tear her off.

GARY. SADIE! You're really beginning to warp the beautiful buzz we had in that photomaton, right?

SADIE. *That buzz gave me about as much charge as a peanut butter sandwich.*

MELODY. Oh, rip her off, its spooky.

GARY. (to MAURICE) Look, troll, what is it? Some boob tube show that bugged you? Why don't you just complain to the duty officer in charge of the station?

SADIE. *Oh, jus listen to Eleanor Roosevelt.*

MAURICE. (to GARY) **Not Only the Duty Officer, but also Programme Reception Researchers, Personality Receptionists and TV Relations Officers, ALL have the same legally endorsed speech patterns which are pitched at a certain decorative voltage so that they Cannot Ever release the Electrostatic Charge they've built up in you the night before.** (He resumes) **It's got to be done like this.**

GARY. Seems a bit like praying.

MAURICE. **Not at all. TZZZZZZZAAAAAAHHHH! I'm getting my head out as an electromagnet to deflect the cathode rays. I'm setting up a smoothing cycle to damp down their energy fields. I'm sending out highly concentrated protein flux via various psychic rheostats to block them off, so shutup because I don't want you to abort any of my discharge mechanisms.** (Flicking his hands faster) **TZAAAAAAH! TZAAAAAH! These are the details omitted. Bio-photogalvanic reduction of Perowne 200 amperes.**

SADIE. *(vibrating her hands in time with MAURICE'S) THESE ARE THE DETAILS OMITTED!*

MAURICE. (mechanical chant, high speed) **FUCKIN MOB IN NEPAL, now working on a Version of the**

Absolute Mind, i.e. En-Soph of the Cabbala, Trans-finite Sabbath of the Eternity, Interlocking Dharmad-hati World Soul, and the Unfrequented Frequency, but YOU, Newscaster Cunt, and eye-contact-pattern-sludge, you DISMANTLED THAT, and parts of Perowne went out with it too ...

MELODY. Whooops! the Cosmic Consciousness Freak Strikes Again.

GARY. (pointing at SADIE) Yeah, I thought they'd given you JABS for Asian flu.

SADIE. LET HIM DO HIS SHOT!

MELODY. Of what? Groovin on your smashed up mind? Maybe we want some validation too.

SADIE. Let him do his shot. He's into HIS head, (Pointing at PEROWNE) not mine. But if he IS pickin up on my head, I wanta Complete Exegesis. I don't wanta be gouged out of it. I don't want you to gyp me of any of my characteristics.

MELODY. Dig that, she's buckin fa promotion.

GARY. (pointing at MAURICE) He's gonna gyp you of your characteristics before you got to them yourself baby.

SADIE. YEAH! He's StereoChemical Energy! (Flicking her fingers strobing her hands) Right On, Maurice.

MAURICE. (vibrating his hands, and spitting at the mock up tv screen. Rolling his head and eyes) I'm sending out psychic laser beams so that they can never come up with their version of Nepal before they did, or psychometabolize Perowne's vibrations or Impound His Energy on that score, and set up Negative Ion

EXCESS EVEREVER EVER EVER!

And if you don't believe me, turn the television on, while I'm doing this, and you won't be able to understand what's going on.

MELODY. (shouting) Who cares about television? It's all Ted Serios. He can develop pictures on unexposed film, just by thinking. He can develop thoughtographic videotapes by remote control. Every programme is Ted Serios. All you gotta do is kill him. I bet you never heard of him? He got there before you. He's way ahead of you.

(MAURICE's hand movements slow down; they become more and more jerky. He twitches, and contorts his hands and his head)

MAURICE. I can't Operate! (He points at MELODY) I can't operate . . . She's hollowing me out. She's trying to soak up all the fuckin electricity in here. (shouting at MELODY) I KNOW TED SERIOS. Last year with Ted Serios I went to the Wigmore Street Electrolysis Depilation Unwanted Hair Removal Clinic, and I got Twiggy's unwanted eyebrows, and Terence Stamp's armpits, and Bobby Kennedy's nasal clippings, and Elizabeth Taylor's crutch fud, all Put In Here (Pointing to his head) so that PEROWNE could have an Economy Sized TV for easier to deal with. Just cut it off. CUT IT OFF. (He turns back to the screen, and shouts at SADIE) FASTER! FASTER! (SADIE stares at him, then lowers her hands from in front of the screen and moves away) FASTER! FASTER!

(GARY and MELODY laugh at him)

SADIE. (Moving away) Nah, I might get travel sick.

(SADIE goes over to the pinmachine BEAT TIME, and starts playing it. MAURICE follows her)

MAURICE. You're using mental traces of Their limb

movements to go like that.

(MAURICE imitates one of SADIE's gestures, and points at GARY and MELODY. SADIE freezes slightly. MAURICE turns round and looks at PEROWNE, who is slowly emerging from underneath the pink shirt. He untwists it and takes it off his head, smiling)

MAURICE. A Clean Break? Cleared that TV track?

PEROWNE. (smiling, and stretching) I feel good! I liked that! (Standing up and clutching MAURICE) I'll tell you something odd. The English Commercial channel I.T.V. was started at exactly the same time as they withdrew X-Ray machine from shoe shops. (He moves around)

MELODY. (pointing at SADIE) But howdja get so next to HER Maurice, like, you know, you never met her before, an she freaks on all those things you mentioned. TV and that . . . Howdja get so into her?

MAURICE. I masturbated in your favour last Tuesday.

GARY. (to MELODY) looks like we didn't lose that three-way buzz after all.

MELODY. (stares at him, and points at SADIE) Yeah? we lost it.

(MAURICE goes over to MELODY, pulls his cheek away from his jaw and makes cunt slurping noises)

MAURICE. Charver, charver? (MELODY ignores him. Pointing to her crutch) Picks her nose and doesn't hand it round. Charver, charver? (Pulling his cheek in and out, then stopping) I don't want you to earth any of my currents anyway, unless you can earth them all. (Looking up at PEROWNE) Just trying to set up a little sex noise in her head, for you to listen to in case there was any plasma on that score left over by the boy with the heady views.

PEROWNE. Thank you.

MAURICE. (going over to PEROWNE) I've cleared that sex track for you anyway, in another way.

PEROWNE. Yes?

MAURICE. Yes, Last Week, Inner London Sessions. Mrs. Gellot's bastard five year old pointed to me and said "That man grabbed my privates". The judge said to him "If I'd been him, you sex mad little gossoon, I'd have cut them off and pickled them in aspic like St. Paul. So, Shove." (To PEROWNE) A Clean Break?

PEROWNE. A clean break. (He smiles)

GARY. (moving towards PEROWNE) Don't you ever get like ... Stump hallucinations? When Maurice has amputated all these areas of your personality, right? Do you ever get stump hallucinations?

PEROWNE. Slight tingling at the nerve endings, nothing more.

MAURICE. Ha! (Then he points at GARY, and looking at MELODY) You go with him? he'd rob his own granny and then scratch her fanny on the way out for a bit of skin.

GARY. Hey! I've hit it now! I've just picked up on his True lick. He's Hurtin Fa Pussy, Melody. Whatcha gonna do about it? Sex Terrorist!

MELODY. Look Maurice, lemme trim your head on one thing. If I ever get an itchy snatch, right, he does a bit of Vacuum talking, and he raises my skin to the same level as the itch, and he cures me of it for ever. Dig?

MAURICE. I don't Need that, you see. I was sold fifteen thousand sticky second hand comes, Wandsworth Registry Office, 1959, and I had to keep her stench on my rod for five years after she died in order to combat Hugh Hefner and all the other sex revolution

41

Stalinists.

(Watching PEROWNE moving free, and grabbing him)

Look at him! Quite a few more people than me like him too, because he's trained his mouth to go up at the corners instead of down, which cost him seven amps, but he's making up for it by spreading himself very thin.

(PEROWNE smiles)

GARY. (to PEROWNE) Do you like Americans?

PEROWNE. Five years ago you would still impress them by show-ing them a reproduction of Van Gogh. Two years ago you had to show them the real thing. Now you have to give them his ear.

MAURICE. See! See! I switched him fit! (He disappears)

GARY. (moving towards PEROWNE, baring his teeth as he speaks) Know what the G.I.'s do now? they take a lot of acid, and acid gives them a very perfect sense of timing, see. Soon as they kill a Cong, they rip off his pants, and plunge their pricks into his ass and they know just the right moment to catch his death throes in order to get their rocks off.

MELODY. Yeah. Everyone's speeding on death. There's a cat laying down this trip now that Cancer's some kind of Pearl being cultivated by Human Oysters.

PEROWNE. What for?

MELODY. I don't know.

GARY. (to PEROWNE) They assassinated the man who invented the nylon stocking which wouldn't run, they assassinated the man who invented the match which you could strike twice, they assassinated the man who invented the permanent light bulb.

SADIE. *If they'd force-fed everyone with a bit of Kennedy's corpse, maybe they'd have cooled out on the others.*

MELODY. America's just a broken down old vending machine and the only thing to do is to kick it and kick it and kick it again.

GARY. (to PEROWNE) Shall I tell you the Great American Secret? Its written into the American Constitution in Invisible Ink. Put a hot iron on it, and you can bring it up. Item: Fellow Americans, always remember that killing fires more of your brain cells than fucking.

SADIE. *Everyone's fixin ta die. They been told Death Is Pure Sensation!*

PEROWNE. So how many people are there left?

GARY. About three. And they're South African. Two men and a woman. They're flashing them through to me right now. On 42nd Street. Two men and a woman. They're so ashamed of what they're doing to the woman, they're killing her. (Closing his eyes) They've killed her. Now they're so ashamed of what they're doing to each other, they're digging her up.

SADIE. *An what are you doing about it?*

MELODY. What are You doing about it? (Pointing at MAURICE) Just Splitting an scoring yourself a Freak!

SADIE. *YEAH! Who else is gonna keep me so spaced out that I can forget about that shitpile and about the two mementoes of that shitpile I was dumb enough to bring with me? A FREAK! A FREAK!*

MELODY. Sadie's really pullin all the vibes out of synch now.

GARY. Yeah. (Going over to PEROWNE) Hey, tell me something. Has Maurice Really straightened out your head? You don't really get a pump out of him do you?

SADIE. *Sure he does. Maurice is satirising attitudes which haven't yet arisen.*

GARY. Yeah, an if the bomb goes off, make sure you get higher than the bomb. We know.

MELODY. (moving over to PEROWNE) No, what's he really do for you? Because I get the feeling you're gonna put him down very soon. Just the way your face changes, when he comes on . . . Little muscles moving, then you cancel it out very quickly with a little smile . . .

GARY. That's called "Intermittent Reinforcement," that's the strongest schedule for keepin behaviour going. Any behaviour you want.

MELODY. Hey! You're a Control Freak! Come here Control Freak!

(They grab hold of each other)

PEROWNE. (to SADIE) Why did you leave?

SADIE. *They've just discovered that dead black flesh is very rich in uranium isotopes. That's why.*

PEROWNE. (stares at her) Americans. I don't know about Americans. They talk about meaningful relationships all the time, when you know that the most meaningful relationship they can conceive of is the relationship between the murderer and his victim . . .

SADIE. *Mmmmn.*

(GARY and MELODY are clustered together,

(MAURICE reappears and goes over to them)

MAURICE. I was completely dehydrated once, and my body was so dry that I doubled the capacitance of my plasma membranes and excitory fibres. I built up a huge surface charge of static electricity. I could lay my hands on Perowne's head and wads of hair would come out by simple electrostatic action.

GARY. Ha!

MELODY. Hey, remember little Frankie?

GARY. Oh yeah, tell him about little Frankie.

MELODY. He pissed on an electric fence once, an his voice never broke.

MAURICE. Come here, come here. You were thinking about the police ten seconds ago, right? Now, my electricity's been PROVED, you see. It's down to the collagen in the bone, and under shearing stress, the cross linkages in the chain molecules of the collagen will result in a displacement of electric charge. NOW, if you're HOLDING, you know?

MELODY. Like, like dope?

MAURICE. Anything like that. And the Police is coming towards you along the street, you put your hands like this (He holds his hands together away from his body, in a ring) and they won't Dare accost you. Because it's alchemy. It forms a Circuit. An insulated circuit. Skin wavelengths of five to twenty mu. And they won't Dare accost you, because you're not giving them any Base Terminal to convert your currents to their frequency . . .

MELODY. What about your Head, that's a Base Terminal isn't it?

GARY. No cop that I ever met went on a head trip.

MELODY. Ha.

MAURICE. **They won't dare accost you (Separating his hands) unless you break the circuit, and then you get your collar felt.**

MELODY. Hey, that's Beautiful!

GARY. A Fairy Ring to Fuck the Fuzz!

(MAURICE goes over to PEROWNE and holds his hand. GARY puts his hands round MELODY's waist, and forms a circuit. He squeezes her, kisses her. SADIE stares at them)

SADIE. *Try it out in Chicago, sagnuts. Look at it (Pointing at them) That's the Seed Shit. That's the Start of the Whole Poison. Just that. That little gesture. Oooo oOOOOOooH she's MINE.*

GARY. You wanna get laid again Sadie?

MELODY. (to GARY) You're so stoned you couldn't find your way to her cockpit. Could you?

GARY. Ha. You wanna get laid Sadie?

SADIE. *No thanks. I never do it properly with less than twenty people. I like to spread the load. I like to spread the charge . . .*

GARY. What about Maurice? He's twenty people.

MELODY. He's THIRTY people. Don't hand us that shit, Sadie.

SADIE. *I wouldn't. My shit travels badly.*

(GARY and MELODY rub up against each other ostentatiously)

SADIE. *(moving round them) That's where it was at the whole time. That's the only fuckin flash you been after. Whyntcha go an bury yourselves in a cave for five years an SEW yourselves together?*

GARY. That'd be groovy.

(GARY rubs up and down against MELODY, jerking his pelvis, and then looking provocatively at SADIE)

SADIE. *(advancing on them, and pointing to GARY'S crotch) You really think I need that, don't you? Prick. PRICK!*

MELODY. I think, she's after some binary fission.

SADIE. *Yes, I am. But I'm not getting it from there (Pointing at GARY's crotch). That's a three billion year old con. My vaginal walls were built in Berlin. There's no sensation there. There's no such thing as a vaginal orgasm, dig? That's a three billion year old male supremacist con.*

GARY. Oh, come on, Sadie. What about that time you were telling us where you put some mercury up your cunt, then get on a hammock roll around from side to side until you bring yourself off?

SADIE. *Mercury's got a very high boiling point. Pricks got a very low one.*

(Pointing at MELODY, who's touching GARY's crotch, moving her finger down his thigh, and over his fly)

Look at her, tripping out on that gruesome bit of snail flesh. (To GARY) You really think that when the chips are down, that that's the thing that's gonna finally cool me out. Dontcha? Prick. Prick skyscraper. Prick argument. Prick gun. Prick rocketry. Prick fuckin bullets. Prickadickadildo dontosaurus. Well, dig this, my clitoris is a transistorised prick. Everything's tending towards greater and greater miniaturisation, right? And my clitoris is a security leak from the future. (Pointing at GARY's crotch) So, how much of yours did they trim, kid?

MELODY. He's still got a pretty little lace frill.

SADIE. Yeah? (To GARY) Well, GET INTO IT, an cut the rest off. Bring yourself up to date. Then treat yourself to a sandwich or shove it round the corner up your dirt track where it belongs. I don't need it. MY WHOLE BODY IS A COCK!

MELODY. She's speeding on pussy power again.

GARY. Yeah. Always a nice dry little fuck in that number.

MELODY. You didn't pick up on that, didja Maurice, when you were groovin on her head back there . . .

GARY. No, so now you got it double strength.

SADIE. Ah, stop tryin ta whale the tar outta me. (Horning in on MELODY) All right, so you got a sharp little come-on, you're for integrated toilets or some shit . . . and you're into a little pot ego-loss for decoration, but at Gut level, you're into the same territory-sex-adrenalin bullshit as the stone men who run the insurance companies. Shoot, you're just a bag of meat aintcha, waitin for some john to buy you the right gold doorstep to clean. PAIR BINDING PROPERTY PIGS!

MELODY. I think Sadie's getting a bit paranoid.

GARY. Right, and you know the only thing to do with paranoia? You Ride right into it, just like you'd ride into a skid.

MELODY. Ha.

SADIE. *I dig a bit of paranoia sometimes. It keeps your antennae bright. Where's that oh so groovy little communal buzz you were laying on me, huh? "Up into the air, junior birdmen?" Huh? You were just using me as an in-off for your tacky little sex trips. Fuckheads.*

GARY. Oh, stop comin on like some amphetamine mutant.

SADIE. *You're agents from the abattoir, same as everybody else. You're just Mr and Mrs Jones.*

MELODY. (to MAURICE) Sadie can only experience people through aggression. I hope you're prepared for that.

MAURICE. (separating from PEROWNE, who he's been holding hands with all the time and going over to SADIE) I don't like those two people any more. I thought I liked her, but then she started combing her hair, and I picked up on her comb crackling. She was trying to short circuit some of my transmissions against the tv . . .

SADIE. *Too right she was. They're two tv sets! THEY'RE MEDIA TURDS! Look at this she carries next to her heart. (Ripping a necklace with a plastic picture from MELODY's neck) Who's this? Now who's this?*

MELODY. (separating from GARY) Give it back.

SADIE. *(waving the necklace, catching it and looking at the picture inside) It's Mick Jagger.*

MELODY. Give it back!

SADIE. *It's Mick Jagger. Now the cat that gets him, he's*

really gonna get it off. (To MELODY) MEDIA TURD.

Dig this, Maurice, this cat's had sixteen million teeny bopper orgasms laid on him, so the cat that gets him, an it won't be long now after Altamont, he's really gonna get it off, He's really gonna pick up a heavy duty flash . . . He's really gonna get loaded behind THAT charge when he rips it off.

MELODY. You're Evil Sadie. You're really Evil.

SADIE. Better than being a tv set.

GARY. Can I have that photograph?

SADIE. What for? to track him down? You'll find him.

　　(SILENCE)

MELODY. Shutup. That's how things start.

GARY. You're casting spells Sadie.

MELODY. That's how things get set up.

　　(SILENCE)

SADIE. Brought yourselves down with you negative shit, an now you're lookin for fall guys.

MELODY. Oh come on Sadie. You got the little buzz you came for.

SADIE. (staring at her) What? WHAT? (Prowling round them, touching MAURICE) You leucotomised even the fuckin taste of it before I could get into it. MAURICE? You wanta know the Real reason I left America? Take this: the Bird Man of Alcatraz spent twenty years storing up electricity, and then some jive Hollywood film unit comes along and they throw the switches, and they spend it all in five minutes. They burn him down. They BURN that fucker down. I know who it was. And they're his fuckin agents. Look at him (Pointing to GARY) He's using perforated back scatter left over from the Rosenberg case to operate a facial tic that he's got, to give himself an air of intelligence, but he doesn't acknowledge it, of course he doesn't. He likes to think of himself as an unfrequented frequency. And if he was here now, I'd gut him. Only he isn't because he knows I wouldn't like to do the Rosenbergs any damage . . .

MELODY. HANG ON TO YOUR PLUMAGE MAURICE, SHE'S GONNA STEAL IT ALL!

GARY. Yeah! MINDSWAP! Clickety Clit (Pointing his fingers, and switching one hand across the other) MINDSWAP!

MELODY. Yeah! Some Real Grid Leakage now!

GARY. She's eating out your head Maurice.

MELODY. (cupping her ears) Can you hear a faint hum? Wow. ALTERNATING FIELD VORTICES, AND MINDSWAP!

(SADIE stares at them)

SADIE. KIYYYYYYYYYYYYYYYYYYYYYAAAAAAAAAAAA AAAAAAAAAAAAAAAAHHHHHHHHHHHHHHHH!

GARY. Well. Well, I guess that raises me out.

MELODY. Yeah, me too.

(GARY and MELODY move towards the exit)

MELODY. (holding GARY) Hey, I bring you down?

GARY. I don't know . . . I'm no great judge of distance.

(They leave. SADIE flings the necklace across the floor. She turns to MAURICE)   ·

SADIE.   You got me out of a whole bag, Maurice.

MAURICE.   Yes, but I've only got to rub a few heads and I can get that bag back for you.

SADIE.   I don't want it back. You cleared all my tracks. I finally left Amerikaka. You cleared all my tracks. Yeaaah! I'm goin solo.

MAURICE.   You are hollowing me out. I was clearing Perowne's tracks. (Looking inside the PHOTOMATON) Where's Perowne?

SADIE. (moving towards him) You didn't mind me borrowing some of your freak juice to finally flip them with, did you? Dig what I was doing. I was gathering up All their fuckin vibes into one big greaseball and pitchin them into the No-Osphere, there to be purified and never to descend, You dig that? You like that? Ha.

(MAURICE is standing inside the PHOTOMATON. He clutches the curtain hanging down in front of the PHOTOMATON, and twists it round his neck)

MAURICE.   They're flashing Hitler through to me now. "What's that in the corner of your mouth", I said. "Quicklime", he says. "It's quicklime." "No, NO, beFORE that", I said. "I don't know the technical word for it", he said.

DIRECT CURRENT

PEROWNE's room. PEROWNE and MAURICE are sitting at a table with some cards in front of them.

Three walls are covered with pictures of personalities, arranged in lines. Like sheets of stamps. About two thousand.

A bank of video-screens.

PEROWNE. (pinching a tacky card several times with his finger and thumb) Do you call these cards? They're more like Farley's rusks.

MAURICE. I shuffled them

PEROWNE. You'd need a cement mixer.

(PEROWNE picks up a newspaper. He stares at it, twitching slightly. MAURICE watches him)

MAURICE. Elizabeth Taylor came round Playland last Tuesday. She asked me to take her round the back. I had to chew her clitoris for seven hours (twitching slightly) I got media rash all over my body.

(PEROWNE looks up at him, smiles)

MAURICE. Gave me an insight into all the media victims all over the world, that did.

PEROWNE. Mmmn.

MAURICE. (almost to himself) Tried to think of her face afterwards. Couldn't get it. I tried to think of her face afterwards to give me a hard-on to fuck someone else with. No good. Couldn't get it. Gone to dust . . .

(PEROWNE smiles)

MAURICE. Just media rash, all over my body.

(SILENCE)

MAURICE. Perowne, I got eighteen different speech tracks, haven't I? I mean I have to have, because of the environmental bombardment. I have to have eighteen different speech tracks ... enough to soak up all the vibration excrement, and acting as psychic rheostat to spare them hitting you all the time.

PEROWNE. Yes.

MAURICE. But I ... I wanted to ...

PEROWNE. Mmmn?

MAURICE. I wanted to ... THERE'S SO MUCH PRINT THROUGH ON THE TRACKS YOU SEE? I wanted to ... I wanted to take the edge off it, just a bit. I thought, Maurice, you're getting into too many shapes. Like ... here (pointing to his head) I went to see someone.

PEROWNE. Who?

MAURICE. It was getting into too many shapes.

PEROWNE. (leaning forward) That's all right. Nothing wrong in that.

MAURICE. I went to see someone.

PEROWNE. Who?

MAURICE. Someone.

PEROWNE. WHO?

MAURICE. He gets an erection from the vibrations from mental hospitals. He has smoked glass on his car. He likes to have people clocking him twenty four hours a day. He gets a buzz off their eyes, but he's very ashamed of this unprofessional weakness, so, he has smoked glass on his car. (Pause) I smashed my fist through his car window once. Got lampblack all over my sleeve.

PEROWNE. Huh. (Goes back to the paper)

MAURICE. Don't go back into that, Perowne. I want to see him. I thought: If I can hollow Him out, I can scotch the whole mechanism, for you, for good. Smash up the whole psychophagic powerhouse. You are who you eat, right? It's going on all the time, all right; but THIS man's got an Omnivorous fuckin appetite. He's a fuckin cannibal. I rang him up.

PEROWNE. Who does he answer the phone to?

MAURICE. Oh, only the most decorative schizos. Only the most picaresque. (Pause) Scots accent. (He points to the wall of photos)

PEROWNE. (glancing at the wall) Oh I know who you mean. He used to work as an underpaid leucotomist in Glasgow.

MAURICE. Right. Scots accent. I said: "How many patients you steal that Scots accent off? Pay them all back." "Your voices are shortening your life," he said. "So's yours," I said, "and there's more people propping up your voice, poor sods, so your voice is shortening my life at double strength."

PEROWNE. Ha. Then what?

MAURICE. (Scots accent) "Come round anyway, we'll have a pilot lunch." Couple of dog rolls and a raw wimpy. "We'll lop off some of your extensions." Now I could have used a certain combinations of words to buzz-saw his medulla then, an leucotomise him completely. But at that point it would have been too early, and it'd have left a few scraps over for his doubles to live off. I had to hollow him out completely.

PEROWNE. So you went around?

MAURICE. (nods) "Well what started it off," he said. Well, doctor, I said. It doesn't feel like me talking. It's not me interested in talking, you know, so to an extent its not me talking. And I've got to get rid of it, haven't I? (Winking at PEROWNE) It's a pony tail haircut inside me talking.

PEROWNE. That must have touched him where he liked it.

MAURICE. YEAH! he almost CAME. "It's NOT," he said, "you are talking in response to my version of you."

I've got beyond that years back, I said.

"You're not," he said. "Look (MAURICE stands up) What you are is based on my totalisation of you. My totalisation of you, fed back into you, is what you are."

"Look at it now," he said, "there's an escalation of totalisations (MAURICE raises his left hand) Your totalisation of Me, (MAURICE raises his right hand) My totalisation of You (raising his left hand higher) Your totalisation of Me (raising his right hand higher) My totalisation of Your META Self (raising his left hand higher) Your totalisation of My META Self (raising his right hand higher bringing his left hand level with it and slapping his hands violently together) Exactly, I said, and I'm beyond that. Stop trying to verb me up, because what you say doesn't last any longer than the length which you take to say it, Whereas what I say, I'm converting into protein molecules, tied to the backs of neutrinos, going Straight through you and coming out the other side. I had your mind in 1935, and it was a messy little fuck then. Sod your totalisations. There are too many people in London with their trouser pockets all joined together and you're just adding to the mess. GIVE ME THE JUICE.

"The concept of cure," he said, "is very outmoded."

CURE? I want the juice.

"We're trying to help you to hang on to what may be a very precious experience. Electric shock treatment, if that's what you're referring to, is only used by the Sergeant Majors of the industry. We're Officer Class . . . "

And all this time, Perowne, he's marching round the inside of my head, grabbing every bit of electricity he can lay his hands on.

PEROWNE. Stealing his patients best ideas to give his trips a little local colour.

MAURICE. THAT'S YOUR MAN! He's the root virus. He's the terminal Adjustive psychologist. But he still doesn't acknowledge them . . . his bastard patients are put down as "D" or "F.M." or Occasionally "Arthur", whereas he has his Own name come up fifteen times in the credits.

"Oh, so you've read my books?" he said.

"I read your books at source."

"GIVE ME THE JUICE DOCTOR. I like it. I need it. NOW."

He started getting slippery. He wanted to talk to me about sublimation. I said, "How can you ride a bicycle and pull your pudding at the same time, or fight a war? If you could you should be in a fuckin circus. GIVE ME THE JUICE."

He said it was unfashionable: Electro-Convulsive Therapy.

The Last True Mental Fuck on Earth, and you get Puritanical?

He said I should keep listening to him talking. Total voltage of his talk: two volts. "YOU'RE STARVING ME, DOCTOR. I've been graduated. They've been running the Rolling Bones Eamonn Andrews Joe Pyne show off me for seventeen years, and now they're masturbating my electricity into a fuckin nightclub called Electric Circus, Electric Lotus and a pop group called the Electric Grape even fetching my car battery sluggish, and Even a shitty little film POOR COW, poncing off spurious distinctions of Working Class, when they KNOW that anyone who does any work at all is only trying to muscle in on my masturbation fantasy, which is all any work is . . . They're Stealing my electricity to describe THAT Crock of Shit as a Thousand VOLT SHOCKER . . . They're Stealing my electricity, all down the line! SO, Give me the Juice, you bitch."

(PEROWNE smiles)

MAURICE. "You talk too much about electricity," he said.

"WHO STARTED ME OFF?" I said. "Who injected ideas about electricity into the fuckin mental trade? You did, with your fuckin shock machine."

"Not me," he said.

"LOOK, I don't want any pansified inter-departmental squabbles. I want the elctronic tapeworms in my stomach INVESTIGATED. I want Warren Beatty tying his tampax strings to the short hairs of my cunt, I want him INVESTIGATED. I want the wires in my head INVESTIGATED. I want the people in the next room transmitting amnesiac blocks so that I can't tell which thought I'm going to have next, I want them INVESTIGATED. I don't want these landmarks of my flying fuckin sensorium ASSIMILATED by "How Colourfully Allegorical of the Human Condition". I want them INVESTIGATED. Go back to the slab. Get neurological. Hire A.J. Cronin as your scriptwriter. I'll pay. OR, GIVE ME THE FUCKIN JUICE!"

PEROWNE. Then what?

MAURICE. He was pacing up and down, pacing up and down. Then he stood over me. Implying that I could have some of the lustre reflected from his white coat.

PEROWNE. In exchange for what?

MAURICE. ANYthing . . . anything. He's always on the fuckin sleeve. But I'd really started to gut him now. He was pacing up and down. I was saying things like: You see, doctor, I'm very grateful for the E.C.T. If it wasn't for the Electro-Shock Therapy, I'd never have had the technical qualifications for that job in Play-Land, would I? Ha. I was running him flat. He left the room.

PEROWNE. Did he come back in?

MAURICE. Yeah, but while he was out, I thought, well, why don't I give him something to help him go Straight? So I stood up and had a little pee in the sugar bowl. The pink spot, right? in the urine of every schizophrenic. DIMETHOXYPHENYLATHYLAMIDE. He comes back in. He's a bit edgy. "GIVE ME THE JUICE, DOCTOR."

"Well," he says, "we've got some . . . some Stuff."

"Stuff?"

"Yes, sometimes if I'm in a corner, I find that . . . "

And he's holding it out to me on a little bit of blotting paper. "STUFF? You tried to give that to Tuffnell last week, didn't you? And you remember what he said to you? He said I've been sufficiently attentive to death's sublimations throughout my life not to need an early warning system. STUFF? That corner you mentioned is one shape at five o'clock and another shape entirely at five past. I don't need your stuff to make me realise that. And I know exactly how it would go down: standing behind me with your Tibetan machine gun saying GO ON Be Introspective, Go on, Nows Your Total Cosmic Chance. STUFF???? I want the spirochaete, not the symptoms. GIVE ME THE JUICE."

PEROWNE. Mmn. You didn't take the stuff?

MAURICE. No, I wanted the juice. What else had he got?

Fuckin verbing people up all his life. I'd run him flat almost. I'd put him right in the fuckin donniker.

PEROWNE. So he had a cup of tea?

MAURICE. He had a cup of tea full of my pee. With sugar. A cup of tea full of my pee, and then he went Right Up the fuckin pictures. All wrapped up in suede and smugness one minute, then suddenly he drops off the chair, kicks his sandals off, heels flying in the air: "I CAN SEE THE SUN—I'M IN THE SUN . . . I'M FRAGMENTING WITH THE SUN . . ." Come on, you can do better than that. "I'm in the sun." Tchah. You'll bankrupt yourself paying for the press cuttings.

"MY COCK IS CORUSCATING SOLAR AUREOLES —I'M SYPHONING OFF THE SUN'S RADIATION AND CORONAL CALORIES 1,000,000 A SECOND AND TYING IT UP TO MY WORLD INFLUENCING MACHINE . . . AAAAAAH HAAA HAAAAA HAAA AA . . . SO WHAT THE HELL DO I NEED YOUR TWENTY WATTS FOR?"

He stepped on his own prick there.

"I'M IN THE SUN—OUT OF MY BODY—ETHERIC DOUBLES IN THE NEW AGE OF LEO! I'M IN THE SUN WITH THE BIRDS OF PARADISE." Bird of paradise? That's a raw wimpy stuck in front of your face. He hadn't eaten any of his pilot lunch. EAT IT UP. Wouldnt. trying to get high on protein deficiency as well. Huh. MacGuinness has been contact high on Oxfam since 1912 . . .

"I'M IN THE SUNNNNNNNN! BINARY POLARISA-TIONS AND EPICYCLICAL PRAXES! CATHECTIC PARADIGMS AND CHANGING WORLD FUNCTION WITH UMBRELLA CONSENSUAL SCHEMES . . . I'VE GOT THE OVER VIEW OF THE META VIEW OF THE MEGA SYNTHESIS!

"You've got nothing. All you've got is a bit of polari picked up from a couple of half-chat existentialists and ex-wobblies.

"I'M IN THE SUNNN!!" Look Icarus, there's no need for that. There's a planetoid called Icarus with orbital eccentricity of point eight three, and its come ninety miles closer since you got on the floor. "I AM THAT PLANET!" Yeah? Its killed two thousand people already with its gravitational pull, earthquakes India China, freak snow storms Arizona, and tidal waves in the Aleutians. When it gets a bit closer It'll suck the sea up 500 foot and drown you and your second-hand visions.

"I'M INNNN THE SUNNNNN." You been mixing with some low lifers. I made the sun a dead letter years back . . .

(Faintly) "I'M IN THE SUNNNNN (Looking down on to the floor)

"I'M
   IN
     THE
       sunnnnnn . . . "

TCHACH. Give me the fuckin juice.

PEROWNE. Was he in a position to then?

MAURICE. I lopped off all his extensions. He's lying on the floor. He's rubbing his joystick. Trying to set fire to himself. I pulled all the muscles in his head. I stomped him into the carpet. He's not going to eat anyone else.

(Pause)

PEROWNE. Don't you think it left you a bit shop soiled, seeing him?

MAURICE. No. After I seen him, there was so much electricity in my body, the whole telephone exchange went dead.

PEROWNE. What's happened to him now?

MAURICE. Now? He's so fuckin paranoid he's had to
have his eyelids pierced.

(Pause)

I hollowed him out for good, didn't I? I paralysed
that people eater for good.

(MAURICE turns the television on. PEROWNE stares
at MAURICE, smiles slightly, then bends down and
stares at SADIE's suitcase. He takes her pink shirt out,
fondles it, then drapes it over his body, and puts his
hand underneath it. Pointing his finger, he simulates a
nipple, moving under the surface of the material)

PEROWNE. I believe that in Electro Shock Therapy an Alternating
Current is less injurious to the brain than a Direct One,
unless . . . unless one frequently changes the polarity.

(MAURICE stares at him. The television comes on.
The bank of videoscreens start rolling. Volume
wobble. Some heavy psychic static from the wall of
photos)

PEROWNE. WHY DON'T YOU DO SOMETHING ABOUT THAT!
Instead of making philistine jokes about doctors being madder
than their patients.

MAURICE. I DID MORE THAN THAT! PSYCHIATRY
PSYCHOLOGY of any Good is about LOVE, Getting
Close to People through LOVE, and anything that falls
short of that is no Good. And he was 17,000 protein
holograms short of LOVE. Fancy starting a love affair
with "Totalisations of your cathectic meta-selves." The
only psychiatrists of any good are the ones who fuck
with their patients. I went back there two days later
and taught him love. He was still on the floor where
I'd left him, so I ripped off his trousers and rogered
him. I put a sperm bung in his arsehole to keep the
pink spot from coming out. It was the least I could
do.

(PEROWNE contorts his body. The Media Load gets

heavier. The video screens start mounting a surge of news bulletins, and programmes. The Wall of Photos starts humming)

PEROWNE. I SAY, MAURICE! I SAY WHEN ARE YOU GOING TO DO SOMETHING ABOUT THAT! See that TV? That TV causes chromosome damage. See that TV? Listen to it. That miserable version of coherence trying to fire cells in my brain that I dismantled years back.

(Pointing to an image on the screen)

Why don't you infect THAT man with your schizophrenia, with all you subvocal speech patterns, so that he finds it completely impossible to TALK in that residual way? I mean when are you going to mop up all these dead co-ordinate points? WHEN ARE YOU GOING TO MOVE MAURICE? WHEN ARE YOU GOING TO NEUTRALISE ALL THIS So That I Can REALLY take off?

(MAURICE stares at him, then goes over to the radio, takes the back off it, pulls out a valve, and crushes it with his foot)

MAURICE. Fuckin roach. (Pointing at the radio) Whenever I have an expression on my face, he AMENDS it with an expression on his. Worse than a sex maniac. But it never ENDS with him. It never comes to the crunch. He tried to do it then didn't he? But his expression didn't interlock, HA, so he got no purchase on it . . .

PEROWNE. (pointing to the TV) THEY'RE ALTERING MY NEURAL RHYTHMS. THEY'RE PULLING THEM INTO SYNCH WITH THEIR NEURAL RHYTHMS. THEY'RE CODING ALL MY CELLS. WHAT ARE YOU DOING ABOUT IT? THE WHOLE ATMOSPHERE NEEDS CLONING. WHAT ARE YOU DOING ABOUT IT???

MAURICE. I've gone down in history before, but I've always come up for a shit and a shave . . . I'll demagnetise it for you, Perowne . . . I'll rub it all off . . . (Skidding round the room, staring and pointing at the screen, splaying his hands towards them. Pointing at one screen) I had to suck Richard Nixon's cock once. In a home movie called "Parental Advice." He had galloping knob rot as well, but I scraped it off, and fed it to the mice. After that he put us all on double bubble, so I thanked him for it and set about his wife. A clean break?

PEROWNE. I can't feel ANYTHING. When are you going to move? (pointing at another image on the screens) Look at HER!

MAURICE. Tchach. That oscillating dumb show and demobilised skin pageantry has been on my back since 1951, trying to pull the carpet from under my feet. Know what she's really saying, Perowne? "I'm not working for the International Stench Factory. I'm not pulling the carpet from underneath your feet everywhere you tread." NO, because she's fuckin wearing it out. Oh, "Nobody understands me," she says . . . (Pointing at the screen. Still image of Virna Lisi) But she still carries on with disseminating what they're told by law to call their filthy unnapproachability . . . (Turning to PEROWNE) Ha. That rub her off for you? THAT RUB HER OFF?

(PEROWNE makes no response. MAURICE turns off all the tvs and video screens)

I'm wearing out all her electrical movements now Perowne. I'm wearing out all her facial movements. Watch inside my head. I'm fuckin slamming her. I'm spreading out her fuckin resonance. I'm fuckin cauterising her bio-electrically.

(PEROWNE stands up, twitching still, picking up on the media. Twitching then looking at MAURICE. SADIE comes into the Room. She moves towards her suitcase. PEROWNE smiles at her. Cools out immediately)

PEROWNE. (to MAURICE) Why don't you turn your mind into a neutrino trap? Neutrino's carry no electric charge.

MAURICE. (scowling) A lead wall twenty light years thick has only got fifty fifty chance of trapping a neutrino, so that is handy. (Pointing to the wall of photos, now silent, and the bank of screens) Everytime I slash their tentacles, You flash through some More people to me, and I have to scrape the mess off.

(PEROWNE stares at him, then shrugs his shoulders)

Hitler had to eat his own shit, to stop rival black magicians getting hold of it, and all his nail parings and all his hair cuttings. Why can't you be that tidy?

PEROWNE. What are you talking about?

MAURICE. (pointing to the wall of photos, the TVs and the radio) ALL THAT, AND ALL THAT, AND ALL THAT!

PEROWNE. I don't know. I never look at them. It's a kind of miscegenation.

MAURICE. Yeah, an part of your phone numbers unlisted. Never look at them (To SADIE) HE'S FUCKIN PARALYSED BY THEM. Perowne's trying to rat on me.

(SADIE stares at him)

I've given you enough planks to walk on.

(MAURICE moves towards the door)

PEROWNE. (to SADIE) Maurice was talking about his mind. Maurice's mind is totally porous.

MAURICE. Poor as piss.

(He stares at PEROWNE, and then leaves the room. PEROWNE folds up the newspaper on the table, and then goes over to the pile of newspapers in the corner, puts it on top of the pile and replaces the large metal magnet that belongs on top of them)

SADIE. Why don't you just buy heavier newspapers?

(SADIE looks at the shirt PEROWNE has been fondling, & puts it back into the suitcase)

PEROWNE. I must say. I like your shirt.

(SADIE twists a loose flap of the shirt she has on. Not
knowing whether PEROWNE is referring to this or the
one in the bag. She twists a loose flap of the shirt,
almost edgily, furls and unfurls it round her finger.
Tucks it back in. PEROWNE goes over to SADIE,
pulls the flap of shirt out, smooths out the wrinkles,
tucks it back in)

*SADIE. I LIKE YOUR SHIRT? What's that? My feedback
loops have gotten a little bit more selective than that.
"I like your shirt?" Didn't you know: any personal-
isation paralyses the system for at least three seconds
(She counts a two second pause) I like my shirt.
(Laughs)*

**PEROWNE. (smiles, then looks towards the door, and then back to
SADIE) Prove your vibrations.**

SADIE. What's that?

**PEROWNE. Somebody said to Maurice the other day: Prove what
you call your vibrations. Maurice said: Tell yourSELF a joke,
and then watch everyone around you laughing.**

*SADIE. Ha. Maurice's mind can get into anything. Every
fuckin word he says is like a joint. You live with him
or something?*

(SADIE walks around the room, taking in the TVs,
and then the Wall of Photos)

*Sheeeeit, LOOK AT THAT! Wow. That really taps the
needle. It's a Mandala, right?*

(PEROWNE makes no response, seeing MAURICE
come back in with his fingers curled and ringing his

eyes like spectacles. He crouches and stares at SADIE)

MAURICE. My staring at her is a unified field theory which will account for everything. She can't stare at me because she's not my eye doctor.

SADIE. (staring at him) I got things going for me, right? (She blows at him with her mouth) PHEWT! PHEWT!

(MAURICE leaves. SADIE stares at PEROWNE. PEROWNE looks cowed. SADIE looks back at the wall of photos)

SADIE. Hey, you know, I did this gig in Amsterdam last week, and like one afternoon, we went to this place: The Ann Frank Huis, 263 Prinsengracht. And we went upstairs to the little secret room she had, little achterhuis, when she was hiding from the Nazis, and she had a wall of photos just like that. It has photos of Ray Milland, Sonja Henie, Princess Margaret, Shirley Temple, and Clark Gable, and I thought . . . like that was what was wallpapering the inside of her skull when those groovy ole Nazis came to get her you know, and I was thinking, well I don't mind having a few of those cats inside my head when I'm eating, if that's where they want to be, or even when I'm fucking, but to have that Grade-B tinseltown shit batting round in my head when I'm fixin to DIE . . . No man, no, no, no . . .

PEROWNE. (smiles wanly) Maybe she went to the death camp to kill off all the photos in her head.

SADIE. Whaaaat? Ha. You can't kill them off. With those cats death's just a weak dogma kept up for the sake of appearances. (Staring at the wall more closely) Hey, its really coming through, Perowne. Its a Mandala . . . a Panoptic Mandala of the Zeitgeist Committee . . . Dig this (She stands on the table with her back to the wall arms outstretched) Radiant green light from there (She encloses a group of photos with her left hand),

Radiant red light from up there (She encloses a group of photos above her with her hands) Radiant white light from there (Enclosing a group of photos on the right) I'm in the centre, right? (closing her eyes) Coming through is Wheels, Wheels, OM, Vairocana, Dharmadhatu and the Lion . . . Right?

(PEROWNE stares at her. Nods)

SADIE. (waving her arms in circles) Eastern Section of Mandala of the five Dhyani-Buddhas, and proto-phenomena from the photosphere . . . Tantric symbol of integration . . . Vehicle of Eastern Section: BIRD-MAN! (Opening her eyes) Now, lets see who you got in Eastern Section . . .

PEROWNE. (peering down at the wall) Lindbergh. Its Charles Lindbergh!

SADIE. Lindbergh. Huh. Well, maybe its not a mandala. (Stepping down) It's your current mindpool though, isn't it?

(PEROWNE almost nods)

SADIE. Best place for it. All these silly ass dumb fuckin heads talking about their heads. GET IT ON THE WALL. (Walking around in front of the wall, staring at the photos) What do you think its really like, huh? Proliferating millions and millions of photos of yourself without giving a shit where they land? Maybe they're told that its some kind of cure for cancer. Stops the Real cancer cells from proliferating. Works like sympathetic magic. Like giving jaundice to a yellow bird.

(PEROWNE smiles)

SADIE. (stares at him) Maybe its a new version of the I Ching you've invented, huh? With photos instead of yarrow stalks. Throw the photos around every morning; tells you who you're gonna be today. (PEROWNE makes no response) Maybe its just Maurice's old socks which he threw against the wall, an they stuck. (Pointing to a photo) There's a sweaty little charisma coming off that one. (Standing back from the wall) HEY! SHEEEEEEEEIT! SHEEEEEIT! Its really hypodermic. Its really comin through now Perowne. Its beautiful. You know what it is? You know what it is? It's a Cybernetic Model. Its a Flow Chart, you dig? Look, look (Pointing at the wall, section by section of photos) Input, see, autocorrelation, anticipatory feedback, meromorphic functions there, anasmatosing channels there, wave filters, postural loops... A Cybernetic Time Series of Sign Stimuli releasing adaptive patterns of behaviour... (Pointing to the right) then... OUTPUT! (Pointing to Perowne) and AFFECT!

PEROWNE. You could take it as a cybernetic model if you like.

SADIE. *Its a bit big though. You know you could have all these circuits on a silicon chip an just carry it round with you in your pocket. (Looking back at the wall) And you got a lot of schmocky parameters set up. (Tracing a line through about eight photos) See this one? Look at the whiteness of their teeth. People's teeth getting whiter and whiter and whiter... (Reaching the end of the line) and look at HIS teeth? We don't NEED teeth any more, you dig. Couple of years time all the food'll be predigested and pre-shat, an people's teeth now are falling out in anticipation of that. So you shouldn't have a trajectory like this set up. Its anti-eugenic. Besides, you never been sucked off by a woman with no teeth, or a baby?*

(PEROWNE stares at her, then looks at the wall)

PEROWNE. I did... I did half think of it as a cybernetic model. Lets see who you've... lets see who you've got in Input Section. Marilyn Monroe.

SADIE.   Yeah, she's Input. She's Basic Basic.

PEROWNE. (pointing along to the right, tracing a line) But then the Rot sets in. A kind of inverse Doppler effect. The original imprint is defaced, and you get about Forty randomised functions trying to restimulate a need that's already been exhausted by Marilyn Monroe . . .

SADIE. THAT'S RIGHT! *(Pointing to the wall) Carroll Baker, Sandra Milo, Anita Ekberg, Virna Lisi, Sharon Tate, Edie Adams, Barbara Loden, Kathy Kirby, Diana Dors, Jayne Mansfield . . .*

PEROWNE. Servo-mechanisms which tend to over-correct the whole mechanism (to conceal their origin) so that the Whole Mechanism no longer proceeds towards the target area, but performs a series of lateral zig zags, and eventually stops all forward progress altogether . . .

SADIE. *KYBERNETIC RUNAWAY! Hey, I'm getting in on your trip, right? (PEROWNE makes no response) But dig this, Perowne. Maybe she farmed herself out to those bitches, DELIBERATELY, Marilyn Monroe. To SPREAD THE LOAD . . .*

(PEROWNE smiles—then moves with SADIE towards another section)

PEROWNE. You get the . . . the same thing here, I suppose—Input section, you get . . . (Pointing at a photo) Wittgenstein . . . then (Tracing a line with his finger through the photos) then the breakdown of the original imprint into random functions . . . Random noise.

SADIE. *Wittgenstein, (Snapping her fingers) He was a big philosophical connection, right? Wrote the Tractatus, right. I remember. Proposition 43: "The word 'fuck' is a picture of fucking." Right?*

PEROWNE. (smiles) But the man himself left it unsigned.

SADIE. *Too bad. But getting back into your trip you got Wittgenstein in Input. Pure. But then these little cats, this Ayer, this Quine, (Pointing at photos) this Ryle, this Chomsky, this Strawson . . . these little, little cats, they SOLD Wittgenstein's Tractatus to the Daily News. They dismantled Wittgenstein's little thoughtkit, which he packed so tight, and it got syphoned off into the receptors of thirteen stagnant behaviourist clerks. SHEEEEEIT. Look at it. Ha (She sways in front of the wall) Ha. ALL THE PSYCHIC CAPITALISTS IN ONE GHETTO! (Turning round to PEROWNE) There's gotta be some economy, no? Who's running the economy?*

PEROWNE. YES. A lot of the circuitry's overloaded, and I find it . . . (twisting) I find it . . .

SADIE. *Solid! there's gotta be some economy. Look at it (Closer to the wall) Tom Jones . . . see? Cooked-down version of Sam Cook and Otis Redding (Tears down the photo of Tom Jones) Bye bye Thomas. (Studying wall) How many times does Donovan go into Bob Dylan? Bye bye Donovan (Tears down photo) How many times does Dylan go into Woody Guthrie? (Tears down photo) Bye Bye Dylan. (Studying wall) The Beatles. You can't smoke the Beatles (Tears down photo. Studying wall) Huh. Mary Baker Eddy? Neutralised version of P.P. Quimby. (PEROWNE looks puzzled) Quimby? You never heard of Quimby? He was some cat, Quimby. He said to a patient once: If I as a typical doctor tell you that you have congestion of the lungs, I impart my belief to you by a deposit of MATTER in the form of words . . . If you eat my belief, it goes to form the disease. The belief grows, comes forth, and at last takes the form of pressure across the chest.*

PEROWNE. Huh.

SADIE. *Bye Bye Mary Baker (Tears down photo) Shall I go on?*

(PEROWNE smiles, nods)

Elvis Presley, sanforised version of Arthur "Big Boy"
Crudup (Tears down photo) Marshall McLuhan,
Readers Digest version of William Burroughs. Bye bye
Marshall (Tears down photo. Moves along the wall).
Here's Fletcher Henderson, still being fraudulently
restimulated by Benny Goodman. (Tears down photo)
So long Bennie. (Pointing) Emperor Roscoe.
Stationary version of Murray the K. Twiggy.
Dehydrated re-run of Jean Shrimpton. R.D. Laing.
Haight-Ashbury Xerox of Harry Stack Sullivan. Bye
Bye R.D. (Turning to PEROWNE) Doctor Harry Stack
was on the same horrible trip, dig, but at least he kept
his exhibits in better condition. (Tears down photo)

PEROWNE. (Smiling) He may have had better exhibits.

SADIE.   Yeah. You want me to go on?

PEROWNE. Mmmn.

SADIE.   Dusty fuckin Springfield. How many times does
she go into Baby Washington. Too fuckin many. Take
a walk Dusty. The Maharishi Mahesh Yoga. Fuuuuuck.
He Sold the same mantra word to me, as he Gave to
Ronald Fucking Reagan. Bye bye Bed Bug. (Tears
down photo) Wilhelm Reich, paranoid version of
Count von Reichenbach an his Blue Odic Force. Bye
bye Wilhelm (Tears down photo) Timothy Leary.
Huh! Aleister Crowley was preachin Hash Ecstasy and
distributing Acid, under the name of Anhalonium in
New York in NINETEEN TWELVE, and handing out
DNA cuttings of Eliphas Levi, Roger Bacon, and
Paracelsus to anyone who wanted them, (Tears down
photo) Bye bye Timothy. (SADIE stares at the pile of
photos on the table and the floor) Bye bye, random
noise. (To PEROWNE) Got you some breathing space,
huh? Feel better?

PEROWNE. They're still there.

SADIE. *REALITY AT WHITE HEAT IS HOLINESS!* Yeah. They're still there. So what else do you do with them?

PEROWNE. You could make them non-computable. So that they exceed the memory of the model.

SADIE. *Hey! How?*

PEROWNE. Change their names.

SADIE. *Change their names? They done that already most of them (Pointing) Cyd Charisse, real name Tula Finklea, Susan Shaw, real name Patsy Sloots. Laurence Harvey, real name Larushka Skikne . . .*

PEROWNE. There's not that much difference.

SADIE. *Right! They're not really changing them. I change my fuckin name every time I cut my nails, every time my metabolism runs through, every fuckin thing I say, I change my name. They don't though. Still trying to come on like some fuckin Continuum. CHANGE THEIR NAMES! GOTTA REALLY CHANGE THEIR NAMES! Individualism is wasted on idividuals, right? Ha.*

(PEROWNE stares at her, smiles. SADIE bends down and picks up a photo that she's plucked from the wall. Looks at it)

SADIE. *Now, let's see who's gettin ready to have his Name changed, huh? Who's getting ready to have his Vibration rate changed? (Looking at the photo. Voodoo chant) Doctor R . . . D . . . Laing . . .*

PEROWNE. (in time with SADIE) Doctor R . . . D . . . Laing.

SADIE. *Doctor WHO? Doctor Richard Dover Rover . . . change his name an set up a Blanking Signal, right?*

(Moving her hands over the photo) Richard Rover Dover . . . Who's that? (Casting aside the photo). I don't know. Must have gotten wiped out some place. WITHDRAWN FROM THE ZEITGEIST COMMITTEE. ORIGINAL IMPRINT OF DOCTOR HARRY STACK REINSTATED.

PEROWNE. (looking at the gaps in the wall of photos) IT'S BECOMING A STRATEGIC WAR MAP!

SADIE. *(scuffing through the pile of photos on the floor) Come on now, more prescriptions! What else can you do to kill off all this random noise? All these psychic parasites?*

(PEROWNE picks up a paper from the table)

PEROWNE. Withdraw their feeding grounds. Cut down their pulse length. Render them completely autistic. Kill them. (PEROWNE picks up a photo in the paper and stares at it)

SADIE. *Or FUCKING THEM! Celebrity fucking! that's a strategy to level out the circuitry. (Going over to the wall) Now lets see who I fucked. (Pointing) I fucked her . . . and him, and him, (Pointing) and him. Shit, I could suck his clitoris up one nostril and down the other . . . and Him (Pointing) I fucked him like a stone fox. (Pointing to the photo in the paper PEROWNE is picking at) Is that someone you fucked?*

PEROWNE. No, its a newsreader . . . Reginald Bosanquet.

SADIE. *(standing behind the table) Hey, have you noticed how RANDY those newsreaders have been getting? They used to get to a disaster an put on a nervous little smile, (Cupping her hand, and moving it up and down between her thighs as if jacking off) but now they go: PAN AM AIR CRASH . . . FIVE HUNDRED . . . DEAD!*

PEROWNE. (pinning the photo of the newsreader to the TV set,

and staring at it) Maurice gutted him in Wigmore Street, BUT
HE'S STILL THERE!

SADIE. Who's that?

PEROWNE. The newsreader.

SADIE. Hey, I helped you out with the newsreader
before, remember?

PEROWNE. (staring at the photo) I find that I need about one
micro-kinesically described item of news a month. But This
man is obsessively devaluing the currency. Talking about the
same derelict master minds with their faces daubed in excrement by the newsroom make-up girl, shoved in front of my
face for me to pull the same expressions of disapproval. I mean,
Am I really meant to chew Ian Smith's clitoris every five
seconds? (Pointing at tv) Why do I have to repeat HIS mental
processes?

What does he do, the Newsreader? He takes a collection of
event-radiation modules, initially all separate, and then he
merges them all together. Consequently all my receptors start
merging and I get . . . I get . . .

SADIE. (taking the photo off the front of the tv) Don't
get carried away. I'll strip your gears for you.

PEROWNE. What? I've had my gears stripped on this issue already.
Maurice gutted him in Wigmore Street.

SADIE. Hey, that was a bit showy Perowne.

PEROWNE. Uhuh. They knew he was living here, so they came
round. But Maurice is very fly. He wasn't in. But this man's
wife started shouting at me, and they had to restrain her. Her
name was Pixie . . .

(PEROWNE turns on the video screen, and shows a
picture of the room, the same as now, with a woman
pacing up and down, round Perowne, and then raving)

PEROWNE. She came round. I said: I'm not sure that I really care about you, or your voguish little life.

VIDEO

WOMAN. You're a FASCIST.

PEROWNE. How can I be a fascist when I'm prepared to acquiesce in my own liquidation, at any given moment? That's why Maurice had to slip cancer buds into your husband's tea, or whatever he did.

WOMAN. HE SLASHED HIS FACE AND HIS NECK AND HIS CHEST AND HIS . . .

PEROWNE. I don't care if Maurice drowned your husband in cement, or hung him up to dry on a piece of nervous cheesewire . . .

WOMAN. You're mad.

PEROWNE. Madness is wasted on madmen. Besides, thanks to your husband, my mind's not worth leaving. Maurice—gave him every chance. Did you know that Maurice was tromping ten hours a day in the back yard to combat the psychic damage being done by your husband?

WOMAN. What the hell's tromping?

PEROWNE. It's a deep breathing exercise practised in the West Indies to get more blood into the brain and to flush it out. Your husband is very LOUD you see, especially amplified over TV networks. And some noises actually inhibit physical growth. I should think your husband's noise, spread over the period of his employment as a newsreader, has accounted for about three hundred malformed legs, and seventen cases of goitre. And then before the Tromping, Maurice used to send your husband parcels of poisoned phone calls, delivered by hand. Wouldn't trust the post office, they'd spill them and they'd leak all over the place. Did you ever get them?

WOMAN. YOU'VE GOT NO RESPECT FOR PRIVACY!

PEROWNE. Privacy? Your husband's altering the shape of my face. Privacy? what have we got to deprive you of?

Look Pixie. Your husband is currently posing as my phantom limb, and trying to flatter me by asking me whether he can work the seams in my head which consist entirely of his own waste products.

Let me give you a humorous version of it, Pixie. You see, your husband's technique involves the theft of a facial expression that he used on the Middle East crisis, for announcing the cricket scores. And the Middle East never gets this facial expression back, because your husband is ashamed of being found out. So the cricket scores are then of exactly equal weight to the Middle East crisis.

You say Maurice cut up your husband, All right, he cut up your husband, the newsreader, but lets look at it, micro-kinesically. Your husband may have been using a tone of voice during his encounter with Maurice that he normally squanders on announcements from Vietnam. Every tone of voice should have its own currency, wouldn't you agree? If your husband, the newsreader, had used the tone of voice, the phonemes, that vibrate in your pelvic bones, when he giggles in a French accent and sucks you off, then Maurice wouldn't have cut him up. He'd have taken him round the alley, and pulled his pudding for him. He was imprecise, your husband.

WOMAN. MY HUSBAND IS CLEVERER THAN THAT. HE'S GOT PARALLEL MENTAL TRACKS. HE HAS TO IN HIS JOB.

PEROWNE. Well, Maurice has just knocked one of them out of commission, hasn't he.

SADIE. *Stopped them meeting at infinity. Right on!*

PEROWNE. She starts using her voice very precisely now . . .

WOMAN. I'LL GET MY HUSBAND TO ANNOUNCE YOUR DEATH.

PEROWNE. I've never been able to understand a word your husband's said. All he's ever said to me is: This is the semantic stratum in which you shall live, move and have your being, and if you move out of it, what means have I got to report your death?

(PEROWNE turns off the video screen)

SADIE. *Sheeit. Did Maurice really cut him up? The gouger gouged. What a slimefest. I mean, really that's the same fuckin paranoid bag the newsreader's in. Cutting him up. Did Maurice really cut him up?*

PEROWNE. The news was given a different emphasis when he was in hospital. It was some time ago. Maurice has a friend called Tuffnell who makes videotapes. We can cut ourselves into the news now, instead of cutting up the newsreader.

SADIE. *What effect does that have?*

PEROWNE. I don't know. We only did it once. I think it made me impotent.

SADIE. *Tchah. Newsreaders are only warlocks. They're not the seed shit. (Pointing to the video screen) and all that schtick don't clean up their poxy vibes. I'll get you through to a Real Strategy. Pick any one you want. Any one.*

(PEROWNE stares at her, then smiles. He goes over to the wall, and picks off a photo)

Now, the thing is with these cats is to set up a By Pass Circuit.

(She looks at the photo)

It's the Famous Film Star . . . Stanley Baker. A By Pass Circuit. Right?

(PEROWNE nods)

Now, the other day, I'm walking down the street with Grogan (Gutteral) "Do your own thing, man, do your own thing." "I'll do YOUR little thing, Grogan." Ha. When . . . When down the street, and moving towards us and acting as an Inhibitory Gestalt, comes . . . Stanley Baker. Now this cat's had TWELVE phantom limbs syphoned off him: ZULU, ACCIDENT, EVE, THE GAMES, ROBBERY etcetera etcetera. TWELVE cut-price versions of him are walking the streets, and as he comes towards us, he doesn't know which areas of my personality are subject to which of his affects. So, to stop him disintegrating when he meets us, and Definitely to stop ourselves being confused as to which of his leakages to react to: we decided to eliminate him altogether. We injected ourselves with puromycin which lops off the polypeptide chains, and causes memory synthesis to stop altogether. "Do your own thing," said Grogan as we passed him. Stanley Baker nodded, AND WE FED HIS NOD RIGHT BACK INTO HIM. Then we passed on; restored our memory with saline solution. No affect.

PEROWNE. That's only possible in mice.

SADIE. WHO ELSE DID HE THINK WE WERE? So many of him, so few of us ... coming down the street Twelve Handed. Fuckin primitive situation. Primitive techniques and manipulations called for. The Sea Cucumber's got ejectible intestines ... pheut! some trip that must be ...

PEROWNE. But what did you do exactly?

SADIE. WE FED HIS NOD RIGHT BACK INTO HIM! We set up Anti-Conduction coils so that he couldn't graft his radiated aura onto us, or any of his characteristics, or steal any of ours. We shoved his video current right back up his ass: That's Your Trip Baby So You Stay With It. "And STAN," Grogan shouts after him, "STAN, you Gross Behavioural modulator ... Take this from a fading psycho-cyto-cybernetician ... ITS ALL FEEDBACK, STAN, ALL OF IT. EVERYTHING IS FEDBACK So ... don't START anything, Stan. (Holding up the photo) Zapped him ... Shall I tear him up?

PEROWNE. But why ... Why Stanley Baker ... exactly ...

SADIE. Why Stanley Baker? You mean all these photos are stuck up for no reason? Why Stanley Baker (Slipping her fingers) He made a film based on the Great Train Robbery, right. Well, there was a chance to finally Crap on Money, dig? Call in Ezra Pound as technical adviser and really shit on Money as Energy Token from ten storeys. What happens? Same paralysing con. Same bullshit riff. If you got all that bread, Stan, why not spend it on springing them out of jail? They were revolutionaries. Any menopausal housewife who boosts a frozen chicken liver from the supermarket's a revolutionary. PROPERTY EATS SHIT.

You know the name of the bank in Berlin that's still handling all the Nazi hoards? It's called the Mercke Finke Bank. Straight. An that energy's still circulating. (Waving the photo) So, shall I tear it up? Or shall we open a joint bank account with it?

(PEROWNE smiles, nods. Stares at her. Smiles)

SADIE. (casting aside the photo) I'm getting onto your trip, huh?

(PEROWNE smiles. SADIE wanders round the room. Opens a bookcase. She finds a metal stake driven through a pile of books. She takes it out and holds it up)

HEY, WHAT THE FUCK'S THIS?

PEROWNE. Maurice felt that ... that some of the books in here were ... that they were going ... going off ... I hadn't read them. He felt that they were giving off ... that they were going Bad. He drove that rod through them to let out the ... vibrations.

SADIE. Yeah. But aren't you frightened of catching schizophrenia?

PEROWNE. No. I'm frightened of him losing it.

(PEROWNE sits, and stares at the wall of photos. They begin to hum and flash very slightly, then stop. PEROWNE twitches a little, then stops)

SADIE. (moving closer to him) You know, five years time, there won't be any problem of this fuckin psychic capitalism.

PEROWNE. No? why not?

SADIE. Cybersex. Set up directional electrodes, X-Ray Thermal Videos, MeatHeat pickup guns ... Set em all up outside Bucking-ham Palace, the White House, Apple, R.C.A., Ten Downing Street, wherever. Make a 5-D 8-track Flesh Reception Movie of them all Fucking. Then you turn it into a cassette, slot it into your Cybersex module at home and you Can Have Them! And then when any of these cats try to lay their horrible little one way trips on you, you can say: Baby, I have had Your True Juice. All of it! What is this surface shit you're handing me?

PEROWNE. (laughs slightly, then catches himself) But what do you do until then?

SADIE. Do what you want. Dig what you got there (Pointing to the wall) You got a Total Map of Personality Radiation. You gotta Cosmic Metabolism there which you can adjust to give you any fuckin flash you want. Too much adrenalin comin through. ZAP IT OUT! Too much sex energy coming through? ZAP IT OUT.

(SADIE takes two photos off the wall, and lays them on top of each other, face inwards. She splays her fingers, and rubs the photos together hard and fast)

Fucky! Fucky! Fuck! Fuck! SUCKY! FUCKY! SUCKY! FUCKY!

RUBBIN YOU DRY (Quickly looking at the photos)

MIA FARROW—RUBBING YOU DRY AS A WITCHES TIT! JOHN WAYNE—NEVER GONNA BE ABLE TO LAY YOUR GRADE BE SEX ENERGY ON ME AGAIN. NEVER BE ABLE TO SYPHON ME OFF AGAIN WITH YOUR TEEVEE COCK AND YOUR TEEVEE CUNT.

(Throws down the photos. Laughs. Sits down. PEROWNE stares at her, smiles. More intrigued)

PEROWNE. I like that. I worked briefly with a man called de la

Warr, just before he died. He could diagnose illnesses from photographs. He claimed that if you had a varicose vein, the radiations from the varicose vein would be transferred to the photographic emulsion, and if he put your photograph into an electronic box that he had, a black box, he could detect the varicose veins, or the cancer cells or the gallstones, or whatever disease you had. Every condition has its own radiations. He had a chart of them all. (Getting up and looking at the wall) I never mentioned it to him but I often wondered if it mightn't be possible to work it the other way round. (Forking his fingers and his hand landing on Richard Nixon)

SADIE. *Hey, I really did hit your trip! And make all these cats sick, right? Just by treating their photos! (Going over to the wall and pointing) Zap! you gotta period baby. Zap! you're white! Zap! you're black! Zap! you got hepatitis. Zap! you're never gonna come in my brain again.*

(PEROWNE smiles, then sits down again. Awkwardly)

PEROWNE. I suppose Maurice operates like a sort of Black Box. His antennae are right out, you see, right out there. He's at all the points of emission. He's pitched himself into a totally non-cognitive area. He's not distracted by people's eye-contact patterns, how their faces move, what they say. He picks up on their total resonance, and then immediately can compute the anti-dotal wave form and just finish them off, without their knowing if necessary.

SADIE. *Maybe. But Maurice is gonna flip you out soon. The thing to do is to colonise them (Pointing to the wall) before they colonise you. Right? And that's Maurice's big mistake. They've really eaten into Maurice. Maurice has short-circuited, and that's Just what they want. They WANT you to short-circuit, so they can shove another wire up your toes.*

(PEROWNE looks fazed. SADIE gets up, pulls a joint from her pocket, lights it, takes up and then hands it to PEROWNE)

SADIE. *Devon laid this on me before she left.*

PEROWNE. What is it?

SADIE. *Thunderfuck. One taste of this and you're the star of every fuckin movie ever made.*

(PEROWNE takes a drag)

Can send you into psychic spaces where they treat Einstein as the village idiot.

(PEROWNE takes another drag. They are sitting down opposite each other. Staring at each other)

PEROWNE. Have you ever tried astral projection?

SADIE. *Uhuh. Cat I knew in place called Coconut Grove got into that very heavy; an back to Coconut Grove. Hard work though. Big inner scene. Worth it though. Get that together an you can really go down on yourself.*

PEROWNE. I sometimes think that what those ... those people have ... (Gesture towards the wall of photos) is a sort of astral body on the cheap. Mmn? And perhaps that accounts for the sense of cosmic irritation that other people have.

SADIE. *Irritation? Come on, they're bugging the shit out of you. Everyone's famous. Everyone's the star of their own movie in their own heads. That's the only fuckin star system that's worth breaking down.*

PEROWNE. Maurice has done that. Maurice has videotapes of himself playing inside the heads of people he's never met, and vice versa.

SADIE. *Yeah. Maurice can spit at the sun.*

(Silence)

PEROWNE. Maurice can spit at the sun and make it spark.

(SADIE stares at him. PEROWNE gets off his chair, and onto the table, and crawls towards her, lying along the table)

PEROWNE. Your ... facial movements.

SADIE. Yeah?

PEROWNE. At one point I was trying to ... I don't know ... trying to find, you see, some kind of Unified Field Theory of facial movements, eye contact patterns, speech intonations ... so on ... I mean, everything's interconnected, you know. If you drop a bottle of tomato ketchup in Tokyo, ultimately it affects the red gases on Jupiter.

SADIE. Hey, have you got into Ectohormones yet?

PEROWNE. No. What are they?

SADIE. There's this Biochemical Effluvia that's comin out of us the whole time. Pheromone trails. Hexanol transmitters and receptors. Ectohormonal BEAMS, and they may be the TRUE PLOT. There's an Ectohormonal Molecule right, composed of all the ectohormones coming out of all the people on this street, right, and they're LINKED by that biochemical juice, and not by any exchanges of wordshit, or sexshit or whatever shit. So, dig this: Maybe the people in that room up there say, through that wall (Pointing) maybe they're cooking their dinner, and maybe the patterns of ectohormones that's coming out of them is making me sit down in this way. In exactly this way, in order that the biochemical balance of the whole ectohormonal street molecule is kept at the right temperature, or right balance, or right whatever it is that that molecule needs. That's what goes down with ectohormones.

PEROWNE. I like that. It's a bit like Maurice and his electricity though, it's a bit deterministic.

SADIE. *Yeah, you could get strung out on it. (SADIE stares at the wall)*

PEROWNE. (leaning across) Will you shake my hand?

SADIE. *Are you trying to make a meat scene with me?*

PEROWNE. I just want you to shake my hand. Why so much aggression?

(SADIE takes his hand and shakes it)

SADIE. *Sloppy handshake.*

PEROWNE. Yes. Five years ago I'd have shaken it like this.

(He squeezes SADIE's hand and shakes it firmly)

SADIE. *So? you're gettin old, that's all.*

(PEROWNE stands up on his chair, and turns round)

PEROWNE. I'm swivelling round on this chair now.
Just swivelling round.
Quite instinctively,
But I'm setting up some molecular pattern.
I may be acting one out.
I met you.
The molecular pattern accumulates.

It might be that these molecular patterns are Sponsored by the magnetic core, by gravitational fields, by other fields, I don't know.

Maybe they're some sort of safety net, to prevent electro-magnetic deflection. These instinctual patterns.

Because there's only 2033 years before the earth's magnetic

field falls to zero and lets in solar radiation: the Second Ice Age, terrestial inundations, mutations, monsters.

Whatever it is . . . I just feel that these things there (Standing on the chair, pointing at the photos) these people, that they're somehow Weakening this safety net, because they're stealing one's instinctual patterns. THEY'RE STEALING THEM. THEY'RE FORGING THEM. THEY'RE SLOWING THEM UP. THEY'RE SPEEDING THEM UP. THEY'RE REPRODUCING THEM TWENTY TIMES A DAY. THEY'RE UNLOADING YOU. THEY'RE OVERLOADING YOU . . .

You understand how we're upsetting the ecological balance? There's a bacteria in the North Sea which converts carbon dioxide back into oxygen. A fertilizer they're using now, kills it off. We might walk out of this room now, go out into the street, and drop down dead because there's no oxygen.

Now, These People . . . call them FAmous people if you like . . . FAm-e is just a measure of electromagnetic waste . . . these Famous people they're upsetting the ecological balance in exactly the same way as the fertiliser.

It's no accident that film stars are called stars, you know. They use up the magnetic field to the same extent as any asteroid. Every star that surfaces is using up the Behavioural Field of anything from forty to a hundred ordinary people.

Let's say I'm two gauss. You're two gauss. But BARBRA STREISAND is 75 gauss . . . and the BEATLES . . . THE BEATLES are probably a THOUSAND gauss.

SADIE. *Sheeeit, you really got the creeping meatball staked out.*

PEROWNE. It's brain surgery, that's what it is. It's brain surgery, without anaesthetics. The only anaesthetics they offer is more brain surgery.

SADIE. *(Leaping up and facing the wall, shouting) ELEC-TROMAGNETIC SHEISTERS! PREDATORY SEWAGE! FUCKIN MOCK UPS! It takes a hundred and forty eight muscles to frown, and only three to*

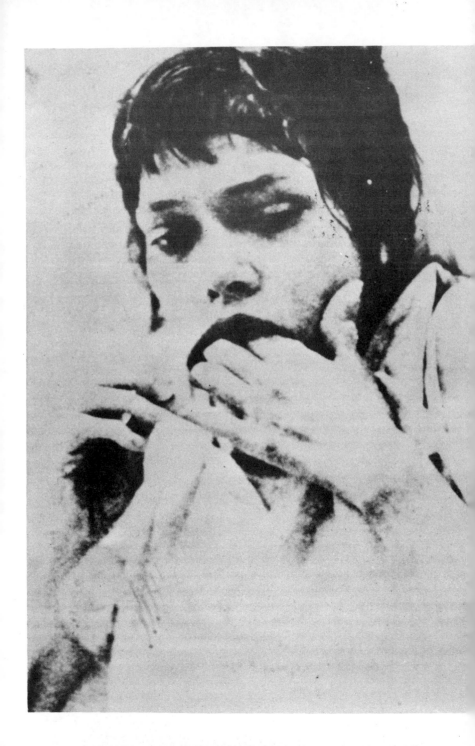

smile, so keep fit and Frown, and man am I Frowning at all you fat cats . . .

PEROWNE. I like that.

SADIE. Come on, shall I kill them all off? And finish off this TV Yoga to give you some breathing space?

PEROWNE. I don't know. I don't know if it's not too late. The sensory assault is too great. It's really a stress situation. It's somehow even too late even to take an attitude to it. Taking an attitude's a form of epilepsy anyway. They want you to take an attitude. They probably use the electricity from your epilepsy.

SADIE. I thought it was Maurice was the fuckin electro-philiac not you. It's not too late. I killed Mick Jagger. I set it up. With a tantric spell.

PEROWNE. Why?

SADIE. He got some karmic debts to pay for, that's why.

Poncing off a few back-dated revolutionary vibes to pay his Hilton Hotel Bill. Writes a song Street Fighting Man, but when it comes to the crunch you know he couldn't fight his way out of a bag of smack.

But don't get me wrong. I'm not going into the Rights and Wrongs, you dig, I'm going into the NEUROLOGY, and the Neurology is this. ALL these psychic capitalists are hustling Feedback all the time, more than anyone else, they're hustling Attention Molecules, and Validation Molecules, and Look at Me molecules, and after a bit those molecules and that feedback gets TOO much for them to process, because they ain't that big enough to accommodate them you dig and so those attention molecules build up inside them, and get Radioactive, start overheating the whole fuckin Network and so those fat cats gotta be DISCHARGED, you dig, they gotta be Detonated. Psychic jiu jitsu. ESP terrorism, or just knock them on the head like rabbits.(Sitting down) Phew, I really hit the seed shit then.

PEROWNE. You came close.

SADIE. Does Maurice get closer than that?

PEROWNE. Maurice does it. He does it in the way he talks. Cholinergic. Adrenergic. Shamanistic. He closes down their transmissions. He generates such an amount of psychic static that they can't get through.

SADIE. Look, I changed my ground crew, when are you gonna change yours? Huh? I'll tell you something. Even if Maurice Could demagnetise you of all your hang-ups, logically, you'd go blind. The magnetic phosphene effect. Human head experiencing changes in the electromagnetic field gets subjective light sensations. No more field, because Maurice has cleaned the slate (indicating the wall and the tvs), no more light. Are you prepared for that? Whenever I see a lame man, I get a sympathetic limp, but whenever I see a blind man, I ignore him.

PEROWNE. (Standing up) Shall I give you some kind of policy statement? I'm trying to automate my mental activity. Trying to get my thoughts to announce their colour, their weight, their valency, in advance of my having to think them. You see. It's much too serious to leave to chance electrical discharges. I'm trying to get some kind of feedforward. I can get close to it on an inner level. I can begin to see it. But I'm trying to steer the technique round to cover everything. All my sensory networks. All my sense perceptors. So that when they're confronted with newspapers, movies, tv and so on, so that they can quantify the charge in advance, before I have to suffer it, so I can arrange the kind of infusion more precisely . . .

SADIE. How?

PEROWNE. Synchronicity. The non-causal connection between events. It's all there with synchronicity. You can often pick up the charge before the event itself has occurred.

SADIE. On a time-reversed trip?

PEROWNE. Yes. Happens at particle level. Happens here. (Points to a photo) Here's a publicity photograph of Virginia Rappe, 1920, with a large bottle. She's spilling a bit of it down her leg. In 1921, she was raped with a large bottle, by Fatty Arbuckle, and died of a ruptured bladder.

Billy Sol Estes, remember him?

SADIE. Big Con man.

PEROWNE. He chose as his theatre of gyping operations a place called Pecos, West Texas. Pecos means Crooked in the Indian language. William Herschel discovered Uranus in 1781. Uranus is 1781 million miles from the sun. Herschel lived until he was 84.01 exactly one Uranian year.

SADIE. So it was all there already. He needn't have

bothered.

PEROWNE. You mentioned Aleister Crowley. He had a lover called Parsons. Parsons tried to resurrect Babylon, by making concoctions of sperm and menstrual fluid. He used to lean over the saucepan chanting: "I shall be blown away on the breath of the father, even as it is prophesied." He was blown away by a rocket explosion in his experimental laboratory in Pasadena in 1952. It's all there with synchronicity. It's a -bit crude. But you can use synchronicity as a sort of geiger counter. (Pause) A sort of early warning system.

SADIE. *Yeah. Did you know this one? Roman Polanski was having dinner at the Playboy Club with a friend Dig? and he and the friend were discussing the death of a mutual friend. Polanski said: Eeny meeny miney mo, who will be the next to go? A few seconds later the phone rang an he was told of the death of his wife.*

PEROWNE. It's a little hard to explain, but somehow having Maurice around . . . it . . . We used to have a physical relationship: that gets things sparking the gap quicker I suppose . . . but somehow having Maurice around enables me to see into synchronicity more clearly. You see, he's moving in an entirely non-cognitive area. He blows all the fuses, so that I can build fuses of a different calibre. Somehow having Maurice . . .

SADIE. *Uhuh. You know they made a film of that? Those Sharon Tate murders, they were set up as a film. When one of them escaped and ran down the drive, they shot him and shot him on camera. They followed the whole thing with portable arc-lights. They forced Jay Sebring to cut his cock off on camera, and shove it in his mouth, on camera . . .*

PEROWNE. What for?

SADIE. *For the porno-film circuit. It was set up as a film to fuck to. It was set up as a jack-off film. Frank Sinatra's paying about thirty thousand dollars a year to keep himself off the death-orgasm film circuit. There are a lot of West Coast Freaks who'd like to jack off with a film of him being shot up, blood squirting . . .*

PEROWNE. Phew.

SADIE. Yeah. Phew. Well, Like you say, sooner or later people gonna get tired of humping your astral body, and they're gonna want to fuck you. (Standing up) Your synchronicity couldn't tell you that. Your precious Maurice couldn't tell you that. What thought are you going to have three thoughts from now? Your Cybernetic Models no good. It SUCKS. It's got no self-consciousness, like all machines. Can't tell you which NEW photos are going to come up next.

PEROWNE. If you had enough photos it could tell you.

SADIE. Don't give me that computer shit. Lot of fuckin symbolism. Give a kid a hammer and suddenly everything needs hammering. (Looking at wall) They're clogging you up. They're really clogging you up. Aren't they? Aren't they? (PEROWNE nods) You need a clean machine.

PEROWNE. A Clean Machine!

SADIE. A clean machine. (He smiles)

(SADIE moves around the wall of photos, splaying her hands, as if warming them on the photos, as if feeling their vibes, looking for the heaviest charge)

More Beatles. You can't smoke the Beatles. (Ripping the photo down) Hey, I'm gonna jack you up Beatles. I'm gonna rip your ass. Cotton candy bullshit. They were the Tonettes for five years, on the biggest grovelling fuckin ego trip ever seen, which everyone's chosen to forget, just because they dropped a couplea caps. Phew, all those main niggers all the way down the line lettin their wee wees get sucked: "Oh man, jes look how dose four nice ofay boys finally gettin our riffs through the customs fo us." Big brain damage repair strategy comin up now Perowne. The biggest I've laid on you. Grab you?

(PEROWNE smiles)

(Chanting) "I am you and you are me and we are all together." Let them eat cake. How many people's nerve cells had to be killed off to put them up there? (Pointing to the wall) I can still smell the phenol.

"COME AND DELEGATE YOUR TRUE HEAT TO US."

No, Kids, give it to Us. No, US, NO, US WE'RE the Sharpest Shitwagon in the Great Needery Node.

THINK of all that energy that went into the Beatlemachine.

THINK if you'd had a Cosmic Energy Transformer when they first surfaced in Hamburg 1960.

THINK what might have been created.

FUUUUCK! Man Powered Flight!, (Flapping her arms) A Nation of Fuckin Harpies. If you can run up 150 foot in a minute, given the right harness. You can do it. You got the energy to fly. I been into it. Could really nail the pig with a machine like that.

But THINK Perowne, what fuckin circuits would have come up if you could have stolen the Beatlemachine's energy.

I mean: REAL BRAIN TO BRAIN CONTACT, instead of just exhausting the energy needed for that by selling the same Fake Chauvinistic Sex Bonds (chant-ing) Ooo-ooOOOO OOH Love Me Do, I Love You... Love Me Do I Love You... Love ME do? When my fuckin revolution comes, people are gonna change into each other fifty times a day to switch themselves fit. Maybe it's already starting. Love Me Do. I Love You. I mean What IS that catatonic little buzz they're pushing out? When some cats are into a Real Erotic Footloose Fuck an Mass Balling in the Streets, to SMASH all those inter-personal hypes...

PEROWNE. What else? What else would have come up if you could have ...

SADIE. Oh man, what else. You could have been your own father, with a post-dated check from the sperm bank. You could have had moving roads. Just get out your deck chair an sit there. No More Fuckin Toxic CARS. There's some real ecological alterations down to cars. Half of my right leg is made from sulphur-dioxide exhaust-waste. And like Traffic NOISE, man, that like sets up an Unresolved Chord in my head, dig? and something really Precise and Manic has to happen to clear that up.

PEROWNE. Such as what, an accident?

SADIE. (breathily) A car accident. Phew!
*   I get my rocks off every time.*

PEROWNE. (closer) And what else, what else would have come up if you could have stolen the Beatlemachine's ...

SADIE. Anti-Gravity waves, Mass Levitation, Logical Language, Ocean Farming, Houses you could squirt out of aerosol cans, wherever you happened to be standing, Centralised Data Storage ...

PEROWNE. Centralised Data Storage!

SADIE. Direct Brain to Computer Construction of any-

thing you want with sub-atomic building blocks:
THINK! SHAZAM (splaying her hands) BEATLES!
THINK! SHAZAM! BOTTLES! THINK! SHAZAM!
BOOSTERS!

(Crumpling the photo)

Oh Beatles. Ha, I'm comin on so strong they can feel
their assholes puckering.

PEROWNE. Didn't you ever think they were rather . . . nice?

SADIE. They pissed me off from the get. I had holo-
graphic beatles that fitted my cunt exactly in 1939.
Ok. I laid a few incandescent little currents on them.
But, shit, I'd like those currents back, and at crippling
interest rates. 5000 million bev energy went into that
Beatle machine, an what came out? One's a bum
comic, one's a society poodle, one's a third class astral
ticket collector, an the other one's makin a little
progress. At one time, they had all the fuckin Power
Freak Juice, and they let it slip from under their ass.
They couldda taken murder off the fuckin statute
book. But they were still into Heroes, an Heroes just
suck up everybody else's energy and then explode. All
these people laying their One Way Unilateral trips on
you. There are more sophisticated
transactions available, dig? The trips I couldda been
on. There's a MUTATIVE BLOCK now, down to all
these . . . these Psychic Knots . . . these . . . If there
wasn't that Block, anyone my age would have
Anderson shelters growin out their shoulder blades;
The Genes would be pickin up on it that quick. And
Earlids that Blink. And . . . And . . . shit a whole lot
more. The GENES are BLOCKED. Blocked by psychic
capitalists heading off all the energy. When my fuckin
revolution comes Everybody in the World's gonna be on
television ALL THE TIME. THEN there's gonna be an
"Information explosion". No more names. No more
signature artists. No more selective newsreader psychosis.
No more selective Beatle psychosis. There's gonna be
TOTAL ACCESS . . . TOTAL ACCESS.

ACCESS... TOTAL ACCESS.

(She slings down the photo, and flops into the chair.)

PEROWNE. What else? What else would have come up, if you'd been in Hamburg, 1960, and stolen the Beatlemachine?

SADIE. *I don't know. I got the visionary cramps. (Looking up at him. Smiling) Didn't think I could come across, did you? Didn't think I could deliver the goods, did you? Lay it all on me, I'll cool you out. I'll bite through all your biopathic armoury. And I can cook up that jive lick of Maurice's anytime you want, but I'm into something much heavier. (SADIE gets up and turns on the television) Now, let's see what goes down here. You should be able to take anything now.*

(SILENCE. The Television comes on. PEROWNE stares at it.)

PEROWNE. America should be put to sleep for a hundred years. America's a psychopath. But psychopaths can still deploy themselves. They can still make strategies, they can still make very careful plots. The thing to do is not to try and Check it, but to Continue the parameter. To combat irrationality with irrationality. To make it entirely schizophrenic. Properly schizophrenic. (Holding out his hand, as if holding a gun. American accent) How am I expected to fire this gun, when it looks like a cabbage? HEY MACK, I CAN'T FIRE THIS GUN, THE TRIGGER'S STARTED MENSTRUATING.

SADIE. *Oh shape up, shape up willya?*

PEROWNE. What shape did you have in mind? (Pointing at the tv) LOOK AT THAT. Posing as my blood brother. I'm not anaemic. Dovetailing his sly wink into my face ...

SADIE. *Come on, don't let the hash smoke you.*

PEROWNE. (Pointing to the tv) Look at that. Can't you feel that?

Mountains of media scar tissue clogging up my ... There's got to be some kind of Media Ecology. There's this giant electronic exo-skeleton groping at the globe, like some hideous totentanz, and fucking it in all the wrong places. Plunging its cock into the globe to syphon it off every five micro-seconds. Plunging its cock into the globe and fucking it IN ALL THE WRONG PLACES. Can't you feel it? CAN'T YOU FEEL IT? MOUNTAINS OF MEDIA SCAR TISSUE TO BE SCRAPED OFF ... MAURICE knows the anti-dotal wave form ... Only Maurice knows the anti-dotal wave form. MAURICE! Maurice is no longer inductive. He can't pick up this any more. You know what he said to me the other day? He said that UFOs have an affinity with electrical installations, and that that was why he worked in the Amusement Arcade because they often flew over and paralysed the machines and let him get off work early.

SADIE. *Huh. Electricity's a fossil fuel.*

PEROWNE. (pointing to the tv) CAN'T YOU FEEL IT? CAN'T YOU FEEL IT? (He begins to writhe) Maurice is no longer inductive. He says that extra-terrestial beings are using mental hospitals as launching pads. He's no longer inductive. He can't pick up this. CAN'T YOU FEEL IT?

SADIE. *It's Maurice that's got into you, not the fuckin machine.*

(PEROWNE stares at the television, twisting his hands, twisting his body)

PEROWNE. They're firing the same cells in my brain there as they fired last Tuesday. All these sensory equations over and over again. They're injecting me. WHERE'S THE TOILET IN MY βRAIN? HOW DO I FLUSH IT? None of these dead sensory equations should be allowed to enter my brain unless they're disposal wrapped. LOOK AT THEM NOW! trying to dilute all my morphisms to a more polite level.

IF IT'S ME IN THERE...
IF IT'S ME IN THERE...
WHEN ARE YOU GOING TO GIVE ME VACANT
POSSESSION?

Look at that expression there (Pointing to the television) he's using all the billing and cooing, nuzzling and sucking now that's gone on on my bed to run that SMILE. I mean fusion of nuclei's apt to pall, isn't it? FUSION OF NUCLEI'S APT TO PALL. Why don't YOU take the load? (SADIE moves back against the wall) PEROWNE turns back to the TV) And now they're wiring up my bed radiation modules to their STOP AND THINK. (Pointing to TV) He's saying STOP AND THINK and using energy from MY BED to say it STOP AND THINK. WHICH OF THE STOPS BETWEEN THEIR SECOND HAND SILENCES ARE THEY TRYING TO STOP ME FROM THINKING ABOUT? Can't you feel it? (The videos are rolling, the wall of photos humming, the sound from the teevees throbbing) Look at it now. They're cutting all the lines of force in all the wrong places. They're putting the conductors in all the wrong places. IT'S A DRIED UP MAGNETIC STORM. WHERE'S THE DISPLACEMENT CURRENT? (he starts rocking his head) WHERE'S THE DISPLACEMENT CURRENT?

SADIE.   (from the other side of the room) Don't look at me.

(PEROWNE contorts his body, falling down in front of the TV., performing a series of myoclonic jerks and akinetic seizures. He has a severe torsional spasm.)

PEROWNE.   AAAAAAAAH AAAAAAAA AAAA AAAAAAAAAAA AAAAH AAAAAAAAA.

(The sounds from the video screens and the wall fade. PEROWNE sits frozen with one hand locked in front of him, one hand locked behind his neck. SADIE stares at him, almost cowering against the wall. MAURICE comes into the room)

MAURICE. (towards PEROWNE, but not seeing him) Your friend Tuffnell's got into my head. Last week he had one foot on the grave, and the other on a bit of orange peel, but now he's onto it. Yesterday, he was only on the bottom rung: People sending him their bad dreams for him to have, and the War Office putting nerve gas in his wallpaper. But Now, he's Right onto it: The Gods using his brain as a telephone exchange and saying fucking fucking fucking all the time to tot it up to Gmm Cos Theta squared. WHO GAVE HIM THE FUCKIN VISA THEN? WHO TOLD HIM WHERE MY HEAD WAS? THE FUCKIN CUNT. HE'S HOLLOWING ME OUT! (To SADIE) HE'S HOLLOWING ME OUT! TUFFNELL'S HOLLOWING ME OUT! CUNT! CUNT!

(MAURICE glances at PEROWNE, and notices his position for the first time, he stares at him, stares back at SADIE, and then walks over to PEROWNE, taking a photo off the wall en route)

MAURICE. (brandishing the photo in front of PEROWNE's face) Gypsy Rose Lee Dead! From telling you whereabouts in your crutch you live. Dead.

(PEROWNE makes no reaction. MAURICE stares at him)

MAURICE. (to SADIE) Did you jack him up like that? Did you? You been over-amping him. I thought you were going to demagnetise him.

(He takes a bone from his pocket, and forcibly opens PEROWNE's mouth and sticks it in across his jaw)

I thought you were going to discharge him. You been over-amping him. (To PEROWNE) Never mind. I can still demagnetise you. I've got a lot of schizophrenia left. Tuffnell didn't hollow me out completely. Ha.

(He goes over to the pile of newspapers, and takes the

large magnet weight from the top of the pile and brings it back to PEROWNE. The TV set in front of PEROWNE is still on)

Ha. I'm gonna switch you fit. HA! I'M GONNA WEE WEE ALL OVER THE TEEVEE, AND DRIVE IT CRAYZEE! SO THAT YOU NEVER HAVE TO MESH WITH IT AGAIN, EVER EVER EVER!

(He pisses all over the television screen, then he takes one of the video mikes and plugs it in to the straight TV, superimposing his own commentary onto the sound coming from the straight TV. And he bends down, with the mike in one hand and the magnet in the other, drawing the magnet across the screen, distorting all the images, gathering them all up, making them swirl and merge with each other, in exploding anamorphic bubbles)

MAURICE. (high—speed—metallic) She's—pointing—to—me—and—strafing—my—tongue—with—her—eyelashes—and—she's—saying—You're—Sitting—Too—Close—To—Me—and—Why's—That?—because—she's—Smashed—up—my—version—of—my—body—1963—toring—off—scabs—like—wet—kleenex—Saying—even—I—know—about—your—Teeth—Mauricio—and—how—they—got—Persistent—Pulp—and—if—you—watch—me—long—enough—I'll—knock—one—out—of—kelter—and—it'll—grow—into—your—head—HA—Glint—in—her—eye—size—of—a—fuckin—cataract——I—said—that—What—you're—saying—is—a—Trumped—up—Deluge—and—Lacerating—Field—Flux—and—I—was—let—Past—that—1959—with—the—aero—crash—even—though—they—wheeled—it—on—as—Porfino—Rubirosa—Playboy—and—hydraulic—lizard—to—say—in—a—car—crash—and—shouting—Where's—My—Fuckin—Handbag—?—When—he—regained—a—bit—of—conscience—about—operating—on—me—decanted—from—the—crash—car—which—

was—impresarioed—as—a—Joke—But—then—I—kicked—him—up—a—space—and—he—was—told—to—go—back—into—into—a—Dead—Set—

(SADIE stares at them, then moves towards them, shouting)

SADIE. THEY'RE NOT RECEIVING YOU

Piece—and—the—bolt—
he—shot—made—a—
tremendous—fuckin—
noise—and—stopped—
him—trying—to—
circumcise—my—skull—
so—that—all—the—hard—
cells—would—form—up—
and—desensitise—and—
also—to—show—the—
strenth—of—his—
operation—on—me—all—
this—time—with—the—
leather—on—his—high—
heels—being—worn—
down—to—the—steel—
peg—But—Even—When—
I'd—got—Past—that—
they're—coming—up—
again—with—his—
blisters—and—his—
breathing—on—them—
long—distance—and—
watching—his—breath—
condense—inside—and—
get—confident—UNTIL—
THEY—GOT—IT—UP—
AGAIN—TO—THE—
LYMPH—RATION—
LAID—DOWN—BY—
THE—1969—AERO—
CRASH . . .

Why—don't—you—just—
find—the—end—of—his—
tether?—They're—saying
saying—to—me—now—I—
said—Somebody's—cut—
it—off—

(MAURICE unplugs the
video mike, puts down
the magnet, and stands
behind PEROWNE,

MAURICE ABSOL-
UTELY NONE OF
THEM! PORFIRO
RUBIROSA'S NOT
RECEIVING YOU
OTHERWISE THERE
WOULDN'T BE
THAT PLASTIC
CUNT SHOP IN
PARK LANE . . .
DIELAN THOMAS
ISN'T RECEIVING
YOU OTHERWISE
THERE WOULDN'T
BE CROWDS OF
SECOND HAND AU-
TO-DESTRUCTIVE
D I O N Y S I A N
D R U N K S W I T H
VOICES LIKE CIG-
ARS TUNING UP
THAT I MET IN
SOHO AN FULHAM
— C H U R C H I L L
H I L L ' S N O T
RECEIVING YOU
OTHERWISE THERE
WOULDN'T BE SIX
HUNDRED CONSER-
V A T I V E POLI-
TICIANS IN YOUR
PARLIAMENT WITH
THEIR HAIR CUT
SHORT BECAUSE
THEY'RE SO PROUD
OF THEIR LOBOT-
OMY SCARS, AN
WATERING DOWN
CHURCHILL-HILL'S
SPEECH PATTERNS
IN ORDER TO
D R O W N T H E
BLACKS AND THE
PAKISTANIS AND

massaging his scalp)

A clean break?

(PEROWNE nods.
MAURICE massages his
shoulders)

*EXTINGUISH THEIR
BEAUTIFULLY
ROLLED JOINTS.
JAYNE MANSFIELD
ISN'T RECEIVING
YOU EVEN
THOUGH SHE WAS
DECAPITATED AND
THEREFORE DOUB-
LED THE AREA OF
HER RECEPTIVE
THRESHOLD. SHE'S
NOT RECEIVING
YOU OTHERWISE
THERE WOULDN'T
BE SWARMS OF
UNCLE TOM
BITCHES CATA-
PULTING THEM-
SELVES INTO THE
UPPER AIRS WITH
YOUR COCK AND
CLEANING THE
SWEAT OFF THEIR
MENTAL LIGA-
MENTS BY RUN-
NING THEM
THROUGH YOUR
ASS . . .*

*THEY'RE
NOT
RECEIVING
YOU ABSOLUTELY
NONE
OF THEM!*

**MAURICE. (taking his hands off PEROWNE's shoulders)
Who brought him off? WHO BROUGHT HIM OFF?**

*SADIE. I brought him off. I brought him off with some
superior techniques to that crap. Well, I was just about
to.*

PEROWNE. You didn't.

MAURICE. WHO BROUGHT HIM OFF?

PEROWNE. It's not a live issue.

MAURICE. She's hollowing me out.

SADIE. *No shit. You schiz are all the same. Signature artists. You want the same feedback as anyone else. Ok, you shat on your ego. You're all over the place. Solid. But it's only to give your super-ego more elbow room. You're still panhandling for validation.*

MAURICE. She's hollowing me out.

SADIE. *Sure I'm hollowing you out. If you wanna work up any kind of communal buzz, how 'else is the game to be played?*

MAURICE. She's hollowing me out.

SADIE. *Yeah, I'm stealing your vibes in relays. Every hour, on the hour I'm stealing your vibes, so that he can factorise the neat little mess that's left.*

MAURICE. Come here. I had a vision three micro-seconds back: I was told the only cure for schizophrenia is to make at least two other people schizophrenic. I've sent Tuffnell up the pictures, so that only leaves one to go. What's your feeling about that?

SADIE. *Not Much. I think you got your work cut out with Perowne. He was pretty freaked out just then, when you weren't here.*

MAURICE. Yeah? That was NOTHING. He's been Training the television set to Give him epileptic fits. (To PEROWNE) You didn't know I knew that did you? (To SADIE) Get him to tell you about it. That's HIS

seal of good housekeeping.

SADIE.   Yeah? (To PEROWNE) That right?

(PEROWNE shrugs his shoulders)

I tied 300 epileptics together once, timed to go off a minute apart. I got a real charge out of it. Set up an E.S.P. card guessing experiment at the same time, and when the last epileptic fired, I'd got 24 of the 25 cards right, it really vamped up the psychic static.

(PEROWNE gets to his feet)

PEROWNE.   They're masked fits. They're not grand mal motorised convulsions. I'm not a pack horse.

SADIE.   Yeah? Junior epilepsy. Only knock down the things you wanta knock down.

PEROWNE.   Nothing stylised.

MAURICE.   Right. No fuckin froth with Perowne.

PEROWNE.   It's custom built for me though. All the right signals are swamped. A few carefully selected focal discharges in the appropriate areas. It's like chess. It leaves no mental traces. (To SADIE) Would you like to understand the mechanics of it? (He goes over to the television and points at it briefly) Newsreader Honeycombe sets the tempo of an auditory and photic pulsed discharge through the centrencephalic temporal-lobe circuit at a frequency which I can match exactly with the 'K' complex of an epileptiform seizure. There's one programme for everybody, of course. And then taking the television as the epileptic aura, I can float anything I want into it and burn them into cancerous dust.

SADIE.   Sheeeit! That's the Heat Death of the Universe. You didn't tell me about that. That's the Total Buzz of the Future, Perowne! That's Home-Made Generation, right? That's Pure electricity. That's your Private By-Pass-Circuit . . . you could wipe anything off the slate with that, no? (To PEROWNE) So what were you grooming me for, huh? (To MAURICE) An you weren't into him at all. "Who brought him off?" He's getting right through without you now Maurice. He's self-discharging.

MAURICE. Not at all. Perowne has his epilepsy to keep up with my electro-shocks. He has the fits and I have the shocks, to level up our energy systems, (i.e. to equalize the phosphocreatine which is lowered in the bloodstream by shocks, and also by fits), so, we're still running at peak to peak amplitude; And in case anything goes wrong, I keep a souped-up version of epilepsy in there (Pointing to his crutch) to level it up. COME ON SADIE WE CUT YOU A LOT OF SLACK. WHAT YOU GOT TO MUSCLE IN ON THAT? HUH? HUH?

SADIE.   I got something to muscle in on that, but Look. I thought you were gonna get me into a Totally New Motivational Bag, dig, of ESP motivation, an you're into the same territory-sex-adrenalin-bullshit, however freaky you've made it look . . . Who brought who off . . . who's hollowing who out, Etecetera. Who's stealing who's psychic zoot suits. Let me cool you out for a start Maurice. I'll tell you where it's at. You know what he was doing when you weren't here just now? He was trying to get ME into the same terminal bag that he's had you in for years. Rappin all that seamless shit. Trying to get me into that, so he'd have a Double Field set up, and two schizoid toilets for his psychic offal. Look at that fuckin wall, Maurice, because he's made you so like them. Look at the way you do your hair. You do your hair the same way as that cat there (pointing to the photo) Perowne's made you eat so many of them you've picked up on their DNA. I'm not gonna Touch you. You're the worst media sludge of them all. (Turning to Perowne) And dig this, Perowne, you CAN'T factorise it. It's a totally non-operational model; you know what the band-width is? It's like that (Holding her finger and thumb with a tiny gap between them) They're all pushing the SAME resonance field. J. Edgar Hoover equals Abbie Hoffman equals Richard Nixon equals Enoch Powell equals Neil Armstrong equals Bob Dylan equals equals equals. Because they ALL got an interest in keeping the SAME resonance field going otherwise they wouldn't be able to jack-off into your head on a one-way trip. I'm not competing with Maurice to see who can trip out on it most, because I got a resonance field stashed in my head that they can't get NO FUCKIN PURCHASE ON and I'll move you into it to cool you out if you like.

MAURICE. Oh poodle off.

PEROWNE. (quietly, staring at SADIE) I can always tell when it's coming. The props to be defaced, erased. I set them all out. Press my eyes (He gazes at SADIE, then presses his eyes) When the little dots, the phosphenes, when they start glowing . . .

SADIE. Oh Come On. STOP TRYIN TA FREAK ME! And take me OUTTA THERE (Pointing at PEROWNE's head); I KNOW! I KNOW! THOSE LITTLE DOTS GOT SUBTITLES WITH SADIE WRITTEN ON! YOU'RE NOT BURNING ME INTO NO CANCEROUS DUST.

MAURICE. Hey, hey, hey. Who's a signature artist? Who's frightened of getting lost in the shuffle? Ha.

SADIE. Sittin roun with a couplea cracker fags gossipin about the brain. I had a sweet tight little high goin, you muthafukkas. YOU BLEW IT, YOU MUTHA-FUKKAS! YOU BLEW IT!

I gotta realign myself

I gotta get the current flowing right. (Picking up some photos from the table and the wall, and rolling them into a tube) Whole earth's got an exoskeletal nervous system. Geodetic. You gotta keep in with that. Terres-

tial currents. I gotta realign myself. (She stands up on the table) I'm gonna get rid of all your teevee heebie jeebies. I'm gonna douse all your negative juice with the only fuckin amnesiac weapon there is. All these freakpuke radiations, makin you like this. I'm gonna Douse them.

(She rips open her fly, and shoves the roll of photos up her cunt)

COME ON IN, NIXON JAGGER HOOVER AND ALL YOU COSMIC MENTAL PATIENTS! COME INTO MY DARK ROOM AN LET ME DEVELOP YOU! COME IN AND RADIATE MY CUNT! YOU REALLY WANT ME TO MERGE WITH THE CREEPING MEATBALL, WELL I AM, WHY AREN'T YOU WATCHING?

(Moving the tube of photos in and out)

I'M SOAKIN UP ALL THE MEDIA RASH THAT'S GIVIN YOU BAD VIBES. I'M LOADING UP ON ALL THEIR FACES, AND ALL THEIR VOICES, AND ALL THEIR IMPRINTS. I'M GOIN RIGHT DOWN ON THEM.

I'M GONNA MASTURBATE EVERYBODY'S RE-VERBERATIONS INTO NEUTRAL. I'M STASHING THEM ALL INTO MY COSMIC SQUELCH CHAM-BER, AND THEN I'M GONNA FIRE MY SWEET ORGONE GUN (Rubbing the photos against her clitoris) AND DOUSE THEM ALL WITH MY AMNESIAC PEARL JUICE!

(She turns round on the table, rubbing harder and harder, then breathing and panting in heavy gasps, gyrating her crutch. PEROWNE is·kneeling down beside the chair, staring up at her. MAURICE watches him, and then moves quickly towards the table, walking round it, looking up at SADIE)

MAURICE. Tchah. They had me masturbating twenty times a day at the Maudsley Clinic to balance their case history books. (Singing) Oh rambling rose, the more you feel it the more it grows. I thought it was my job. Servicing one-armed bandits. Why don't you go over there, Perowne? Give the girl the feeling that she fits-in? Do you want rimming girl? I can put you in touch with some very complicated meat.

(SADIE moves the photos in and out)

She's taking someone's temperature.

PEROWNE. Yes.

MAURICE. (shouting at SADIE) Fancy a gay lick? Perowne's manky teeth have been at the scene of many an untimely accident. COME ON PEROWNE. She's waiting for your big kartzo in her split level cunt.

PEROWNE. SHUT UP.

MAURICE. (staring; quietly) She's trying to decathect my prick. I can feel it growing back up inside me. ITS COMING OUT. ITS COMING OUT. (He sticks his tongue out at SADIE)

PEROWNE. STOP TRYING TO LEVEL OFF THE CHARGE!

MAURICE. WHAT YOU MEAN? SHE'S TRYING TO SCUTTLE ALL THE IMPREGNATIONS IN THIS ROOM! I had to depopulate all those Gadarene corpse photos, and hack fuckin talismens before she could be wheeled on. I staked all this out. She's a fuckin claim jumper.

SADIE. Nrrrraaaah . . . nrrrraaaaa . . . hrrrraaaaaahh!

MAURICE. It won't make any difference you know, what she's doing. I sprayed all those photographs with anti-static lamination.

SADIE. *Nnnnnrrrrraa . . .   nnnrrrrraaaaggggh . . . nrrrraaa aa . . .*

MAURICE. (pointing at SADIE) I'm not taking you any-where. You get travel sick.

SADIE. *I'M SOAKING UP ALL THE MEDIA RASH IN ALL THE REVERBERATIONS AN I'M MERGING ALL THE PHOTOEMULSION EVER AND I'M SEND-ING IT ALL ON A HUGE COSMIC COME MISSION FROM WHICH THEY'LL NEVER RETURN. errraaaa HH . . . NRRRRAAAAAHH . . .*

MAURICE. Tchah. I've got an electric waste basket which shreds things into unreadable strips of one eighth inch. That was part of my Influencing Machine admittedly, but some parts Perowne dismantled and other parts, he Brought Up to Date.

SADIE. *NRRRRAAAA   NNNNNRRAAAAAANNNRRAA AAAAAAAA . . .*

MAURICE. (shouting up at her) LOOK HERE. I AM PEROWNE'S EXPERIMENT IN BEHAVIOURAL SENSATIONALISM! SO STOP THAT. ANYWAY He's got hundreds and hundreds and hundreds, and they're better than a fuckin outboard motor.

SADIE. *(shouting at PEROWNE) I'm gonna demagnetise you at twice the speed of your epilepsy, an forty times the speed of Maurice . . . SO OPEN YOUR CUNT WIDE PEROWNE, I'm really gonna treat you now.*

(PEROWNE looks up and smiles at her. She pumps faster and faster, jamming the soggy roll in and out)

MAURICE. (going close to PEROWNE) It's all right to be indirect, but not in the way she is. You're not going for that are you? That's not doing anything. Maudsley Clinic first time in: they said to me: Why don't you pitch it a bit lower for us? Why don't you stick to

clenching your jaw and rippling your cheek muscles every railing you pass in the street? We won't look. Promise. I said You think I'm going to try it out all right walking, and then get on a fast moving bus and get fuckin lockjaw. If that's all you can cater for, forget it. What's she catering for? (Pointing) WHAT'S SHE CATERING FOR?

SADIE. *Nrrrrraaaah nnnrraaaaaaa nrrrnnnnnnneeeeeeeaagh neeeeeaaaaagh rah rah!*

MAURICE. (to PEROWNE) I was going to chop off some of my fingers today, to intensify my other faculties for you.

(PEROWNE pays no attention to him)

MAURICE. (to SADIE, pointing at PEROWNE) Did he talk you into this? HE wasn't talking to you. He was just putting a bit of scent on your jam rags to make you more tolerable. Doubles, doubles, doubles. I've got doubles everywhere being reconditioned.

SADIE. *(pumping harder)* PULLING TOGETHER ALL THE SPECTRAL LINES. KICKIN OUT ALL THE JAMS!

MAURICE. (pointing at SADIE) She's tearing off certain currents there, then I needed exactly microsecond then . . .

PEROWNE. Quite.

SADIE. *Nrrrraaaa nrrrrraaaaa nrrrrraaaghgh . . .*

MAURICE. (to PEROWNE) You been shooting stuff through me without my knowing. (to SADIE) Perowne opens the newspaper with a scalpel and turns on the TV with rubber gloves because of ingrown mentalisms which he's got which are too good to be true and he doesn't want MUSSED UP.

(MAURICE rolls over on the bed, face down, screws

up the pillows, his foot pounding slowly at the end of the bed)

I'm wearing out Perowne's bed patterns now, which you can't ever get into and demagnetise . . . (Acting out a blowjob) which YOU CAN'T EVER GET INTO.

PEROWNE. I'm glad she can't.

MAURICE. (twisting, to himself) Thing going now where I squeeze my knee (Holds his knee) and I get a stinging pain here (He points to his arm), or on the shoulder-blade, and a LOT of the souped up tensions I got to pick up's traceable to that mechanism, going on now, WHICH SHE'S PONCING OFF.

(He points at SADIE now breathing stertorously, and still pumping)

Breath she caught then was trying to act as a triode valve to similitudinise my thoughts.

PEROWNE. About breath?

(MAURICE stares at him, scowls at him)

SADIE. LEAVE IT ALONE, MAURICE. YOU JUST STAY LOOSE. STAY LOOSE (Facing the bed) BECAUSE I'M GONNA ALIGN MY ATOMS WITH YOURS MAURICE, AND WHEN I GET THEM RIGHT, AN IN THE RIGHT POLARISING FIELD, I'M GONNA PASS STRAIGHT THROUGH YOU, LIKE A DOSE OF SALTS, AND THAT POLARISING FIELD WILL LEAVE YOU VERY VERY VERY COOLED OUT.

MAURICE. (springing up off the bed) COOL? COOL? We've had that necrophiliac nightmare of cool. WHO'S PUTTING THE SOUNDTRACK ONTO COOL, while you're being too beautiful and cool to listen? (to PEROWNE) Look, I built up that hum hum hum in her head that's going on now, and All she's got to slash it to bits with is COOOOL.

SADIE. *(long lithe strokes) Cooling out all the objects in this room. Cooling out all the vibes. Down to the temperature of liquid helium. Coo-ool. Cool Kundalini serpent coiling through my spine colours! Om Sri Maintreya!*

MAURICE. (cupping his ear) She's making fashionable noises now with her middle ear muscles to try and opt me out. Perowne's not getting a buzz off you.

PEROWNE. I think she's becoming highly operational.

MAURICE. LOOOK. I KNOW that state of mind she's in. It's not worth a casual snapshot. Tuffnell was up there last Thursday. "I can hear trees talking to me," he said. "I'm in touch with the vibrations of vegetative life." "Don't let me interrupt a thing," I said. "You won't," he said, "You can't." "You're so right," I said. "Trees" I said, "Who's ever stopped them from working their passage. Trees? They're putting on a proper circus."

SADIE. *NRRRRRRRAAAAANNRRRAAAAA ... Creepin up on all your vibes, Maurice ... nrrrraaa ... nrrrr aaaa ...*

MAURICE. (pointing up at SADIE) Play the same note long enough, cunt says it begins to sound like a tune. WAIT A MINUTE. I know what it is. 'Spine colours?' Wait a minute, I know what it is. Has she gone chemical for you as well? (To SADIE) Have you gone chemical for him as well, to speed him up? She's gone chemical, that's what it is. I was chemical in the fuckin bucket. They used to give me six whites to calm me down, and six reds to make me jerky. I used to put all the reds down the toilet. In the end every lavatory in the building was flushing itself. Oh, look what you've scooped up Perowne, some temporary bug eyed chemical amateur. You been laying a lot of talk on her? Look at her, she's got the jollies. She's wired up, but she's not picking you up. She's been sitting round getting happily wasted.

PEROWNE. SHUTUP! SHUTUP!

(MAURICE scuttles round the table, picking up two photos dropped from SADIE's crutch)

MAURICE. Twenty three menton photons still coming off that one, and some fuckin mush artistry still having to be worn out there (Pointing to the second photo, he moves his face in exorcism of it, then looks at PEROWNE. PEROWNE shrugs his shoulders)

PEROWNE. You lost a lot of power when you went to see that psychiatrist.

SADIE. *I got my piezo-electric transducers really singggg-innggggg now! I'm reading mental masses you didn't know existed Maurice.*

MAURICE. She's as much use as a fart thrashing in a fuckin bottle.

SADIE. *(pumping harder and harder, swivelling all over the table, with the roll of photos) NRRRRRRAAAA AAAAAAAAAA!*

MAURICE. (hysterical) I DIDN'T ASK YOU TO PICKET ALL MY SCABS. How did she get that far into it? Because I started her off. I gave her one of my Julie John Reginald Halliday Crystal Sets made out of their victim's pubic hair. But she can't tune it. SHE CAN'T GET A FUCKIN SOUND OUT OF IT. She's nowhere. (To PEROWNE) SHALL I PULL HER OFF?

PEROWNE. No.

MAURICE. (shouting at SADIE, clawing at the roll of photos, almost crying) GET YOUR POISONOUS CHROMOSOMES OFF MY PICTURES. YOU'RE GONNA MUTATE THEM SO MUCH I'M NEVER

GOING TO BE ABLE TO CATCH UP WITH THEM.

(SADIE laughs, and whirls around the table, pumping the roll of photos in and out, shouting in frenzied little cries, jumping, shrieking and dripping in sweat.)

SADIE. I'm CATCHING UP WITH YOU NOW MAURICE. I'M CLOSING IN ON YOUR FIELD. CAN YOU FEEL ME PRICKLING? CAN YOU FEEL ME FRIZZ-ING YOU UP? I'M ZAPPING RIGHT THROUGH YOUR HEAD NOW MAURICE.

MAURICE. (standing against the wall of photos, holding his crotch, he grinds it like a small boy, starts trembling, and jumping up and down, copying Sadie's gyrations) Look LLOOOOOK LOOOOK YOU DUMB BITCH, IT'S NOTHING TO ME, BECAUSE I'VE HAD IT SET DOWN WITH THE BEATLES GOV-ERNING SOLICITORS, I'M GOING TO BE BURIED WITH MY OWN COCK IN MY OWN FUCKIN MOUTH . . .

SADIE. (jumping and jiving with the roll) Boddhisatva don't come till everyone come! SMASH KARMIC CONGESTION. LOSE IT ALL ITS POWER.

I'M FEEDING YOUR WHOLE SCHIZOID MEDIA RASH CRAP INTO MY CUNT, AN ALL YOUR BEHAVIOURAL PARAMETERS . . . I'M CLIPPING IT OFF WITH MY BIG FAT CUNT PETALS, AND WHEN I TOUCH MY CLITORIS I'M GONNA FIRE IT INTO OUTER SPACE!

(SADIE triggers her clitoris with the roll of photos, and then flops down on the table, shouting FIRE FIRE FIRE FIRE. MAURICE watches her, jerking off, beating his meat, he comes in his pants, his orgasm synchronised with hers. He collapses onto the floor underneath the wall of photos. PEROWNE is sobbing)

(SILENCE)

MAURICE. (moving up slowly, his eyes wide open, he stands up, and stares at SADIE with a wide angle smile) She's hollowed me out. She's hollowed me right out. I feel good. She's . . . I feel very very good. I've got a lot of light in.

(MAURICE moves around the room, collecting his things, his white coat from behind the door. As he moves his gestures seem released, the armoury dismantled. He stares at PEROWNE. PEROWNE watches him edgily, waiting for him to go)

'PEROWNE. Good.

MAURICE. (slowly) Look at you. Psycho-photo-galvanised Me into a fuckin lush, in order to wear out YOUR drinking habits.

PEROWNE. That was a long time ago. I've pitched my diseases higher than that.

MAURICE. Yes, you had me turning into a schiz, in order to stave off your own gig in the googoo house. Well. I don't care. I'm out of it. It's all been knocked on the head. I feel good. I feel very light.

(PEROWNE looks away)

MAURICE. I can tell you now where my head's really been all this time, now I'm shot of you. You thought I was demagnetising you of all your chronic little hang-ups. I wasn't demagnetising you of one. Even when you dropped me for your fuckin epilepsy, I was there, but I was juggling the little dots in front of your eyes to get you onto THEIR frequency. (Pointing at the photos on the wall) See those? I'LL tell you now what those Really are. Those are all Homing Devices. They are Tektites and Space Grass, dropped down by solar winds, as agents for the Saucer People, because they know that those film stars and behavioural tarts can over-magnetise you to the Saucer People's frequency at twice the speed of anything else. Tell me Heisenberg's Uncertainty Principle: Everything's insoluble because whatever's measured is altered by the act of Measuring it. Right?

(PEROWNE stares at him)

MAURICE. (pointing at the photos) That is why the Saucer People only have the very best measuring instruments.

PEROWNE. Oh shutup.

MAURICE. Huh. (Picking some photos off the floor, and tearing some off the wall) I WASN'T DEMAGNET-ISING YOU, I WAS COMPLETELY FUCKIN RADIATING YOU! (Pause) They are very extreme and agile people, the Saucer People. They're breeding Dwarves on this earth now, and have been for thousands of years in preparation of us living on excess gravity of the outer planets. They've been sporing Autistic and Thalidomide children in preparation for when we've delegated all limbs and dead mentalisms to Mega-machines. They've been pumping through people born with webbed hands and feet, in preparation for when we have to circumnavigate the globodurenal ooze of Venus, and they're pumping through people with dermo-optical perception for when the sun gets too bright for our eyes to see. People who are so-called Vegetables from car accidents are being attuned by them to JUST ONE TWITCH OF THE LIFE FORCE, and are keeping it Warm, and rehatching it, and purifying it, and then passing it on to us completely purified. (Standing behind PEROWNE) They're pushing through more Siamese twins now because they know that Siamese twins is the most biologically economic unit. They're pushing through eleven per cent of all men being born with supernumerary nipples for suckling computers. They've been softening people's voices recently, in preparation for the changeover to telepathic communication. They're turning catatonics into Fakirs, preparing us for the limb movements of life on other planets. They're taking measures against over-population, by merging people, and getting out doubles, and then personality units composed of ten people, and Whole Personality Fields Shared. Schizophrenia's just the tip of the iceberg. They're Beautiful people. But they're working in negative time, and we're trying to shit on their time reversed state of being. We're just using their negative time to enable ambitious psycho-sluts to see themselves coming up on the way down. We're trying to shit on that taste of the fourth dimension that they're pumping through, by just using it to see if we can turn an orange inside out without breaking the skin. We've SHAT on their Faustian universe. WE'VE SHAT ON IT, which is why None of the Super-Dwarves, and the Super Autistic-Schizo-Thalidomides that they're Spawning specially for us, in preparation . . . which is why . ., . . WHICH IS WHY NONE OF THEM FIT IN. They reward me sometimes by fetching me back into the original squitting sex noise that hasn't been in my bum since I was ten.

(MAURICE moves around the room slowly, holding his things in his hands. Clutching his white coat. Smiling. He stands at the door. Laughs. He wraps a rubber bandage from a box of his belongings round his head)

I don't have to have any more people's head electricity from now on. (Bending over SADIE) I've got a proper buzz. I'm feeling Light.

(PEROWNE stares at him, wide eyed, then almost jealous. MAURICE leaves. Closes the door. PEROWNE stares at the door, then slowly round the room. SADIE gets up from the table)

SADIE. *Outta sight. Outta sight. (Silence) But he ran you flat, didn't he?*

PEROWNE. Yes.

SADIE. *That's a bummer.*

(She gets up, goes over to her suitcase, and then hands PEROWNE the bottle.)

SADIE. *Why don't you take yourself back to where you*

were before Maurice got into you.

PEROWNE. (drinking) Goes down like cream.

SADIE. Do you really get fits?

(PEROWNE shrugs his shoulders)

I think it's quite common actually, if you stop drinking quite suddenly, to get some kind of arbitrary discharges.

(They sit drinking)

SADIE. (indicating the bottle) Flash him out for you, huh?

(PEROWNE nods.)

SADIE. (staring at him) Still picking up a lot of random noise.

PEROWNE. Mmmn.

SADIE. Gotta cool you right out now. Wanna REal Launch, don't you?

(PEROWNE nods. SADIE takes a scroll out of her case, unrolls it and shows it to PEROWNE. PEROWNE peers at it, reading several phrases aloud to himself.)

PEROWNE. "Homo Sapiens Correctus... Man's position is up-right ... cerebro-spinal fluid ... brain blood volume ... the third eye ... restores the intra cranial pressure ... " Looks like another Utopian heresy.

SADIE. You want me to lay a real taste on you, don't you?

PEROWNE. Yes. I liked you with the photographs just now.

SADIE. What was that. Maybe that was just a little heavy

HOMO SAPIENS CORRECTUS

The Large Mechanism:

I. Man's position is upright. II. Blood is he
vier than cerebrospinal fluid. III. The craniu
seals at the   end of growtl
These three   factors resu
in the loss   of intr
cranial   press
decrea-   sing
brain-   blo
volume: the e
valent   of a mo
ful of blood   is lost to
brain and   is replaced
a corresponding   volume of cerebr
spinal fluid. The Small Mechanism: A ref
by constricting the arteries leading to the rest of t
brain, concentrates the brain bloodvolume in the p
of the brain   which are in ac
(Decreased   brain bloo
lume li-   mits
number   of br
centers   th
can func-   tic
multane-   ous
reduces   the v
of blood di-   rected ir
those centers).   A closed cir
is formed by one's   perception of the
one speaks as one speaks it: perception of the wo

ultaneous with the reflex action that concentrates
brain blood volume in the speaking center; word re-
nition beco-   mes, in turn, the sti-
lus for   the reflex. A
in of   word asso-
tions   establish-
and   main-
ns a   priority
the di-   rection of
n blood   volume to
centers   for speaking,
tening, wri-   ting and reading.
o Loss: The   control of the speaking
ter (and the other word-communication centers) over
coordination of the brain functions is a conditioned
ex which is deconditioned not only when the mea-
g of the word   is lost, but also by
longed   "sugar lack", sin-
e re-   flex action
s to   supply the
ters   with mo-
ergy   as long
he   blood
ains   too little
cose.   The Third Eye:
anation   restores the intra-
nial pressure   which is necessary to
ace the blood lost as the cranium sealed, and all
n centers are again able to function independent-
f the conditioned reflex, still using it for more
tive concentration.

competition to cool Maurice out. I was just playing back his tracks so that he could see where he was at. A real Christ Complex, dig? Christ was too vain to do that. I was just sealing Maurice off. He wasn't into you any more.

PEROWNE. Some of his anti-dotal wave forms were getting a little toxic themselves.

SADIE. Right.

(PEROWNE stares at the scroll, drinking)

PEROWNE. Seems ... rather primitive.

SADIE. (rolling up the scroll) Well, you're into a lot of these mechanisms already, so it might seem primitive. But this would change the vibration rate of every molecule in your head. It's pretty much virgin territory, Perowne. Give you a completely out front life style that no one else'll be able to copy or devalue.

PEROWNE. The Delectable Mountains. What do you mean, 'pretty much virgin territory'?

SADIE. Couplea dutch guys got there before you. But only just recently.

PEROWNE. I've always liked the Dutch. I've never understood how they gave rise to the South African Dutch. On the other hand, I suppose, the only way to convince people of the error of their ways is by drawing close to them.

SADIE. Jesus. Where did that track come from? That track come from before you met Maurice? Listen, don't worry about South Africa; pretty soon we'll be switching from the gold standard to the vibration standard an we'll STARVE them out.

PEROWNE. Get ahead, get a hole. Have you done it?

SADIE. *Howdo you think I stood that jive photo kick just now? All that blood with nowhere to go. Look, rats fed on a diet of ecstasy live longer. You had a good little scene going with Maurice one time, yeah? But you're due for something else.*

PEROWNE. (taking the scroll out of the case, and looking at it again) The Aztecs did it, didn't they? And I think they used to do it a lot in Cornwall, when tin ore fell on the miner's heads: to decompress them. What did you say about the Dutch people ?

SADIE. *It was done all over. Earliest operation known. The Dutch guys?*

PEROWNE. Meningitis?

SADIE. *NO MAN. One of them just got straight up and walked off down the street.*

(PEROWNE smiles)

They did it on a trip. They're spaced out all the time. They just sit round playing the Go Game. Chinese Chess. Lot of counters on the board: Object of the game: Conquer territory. No army can be surrounded or its territory taken so long as it preseves a hole in the middle of the army, a hole covered by no counters. They like the symbolism of it. They see holes everywhere. But you know a lot of the mechanisms already, Perowne. You wouldn't waste the high.

PEROWNE. What do they use for counters in the Go Game? The little discs of bone? They're called RONDELLES aren't they? those little discs of bone that come out of the ...

SADIE. *I told you: there's not enough of them around yet. It's still pretty much virgin territory.*

PEROWNE. (staring at the trephine in the suitcase) Where did you get it? I suppose blind people must have it naturally, I mean when their eyeballs atrophy, more gravitational pressure must act on the brain, through the sockets, and drive the blood into other areas not normally in commission, so that they can . . . so that they can . . .

(SADIE takes the trephine from her suitcase, wrapped in a silk scarf)

SADIE. *Where did I get it? I went moppin last week. I levitated it from the Hunter Museum, Royal College of Surgeons, Lincolns Inn Fields. (Unwrapping it) Other areas? Sure. Undreamt-of areas. Blind people. You're right. They can hear lamp-posts coming, on quiet streets, they got their pineal stalk, the only unpaired gland in the body, traditional telepathic centre in occult thought, filled with brain sand . . . and they got it responding to unknown light quanta, through having something like this. (She unlocks the two parts of the trephine)*

PEROWNE. Are you going to kill me with that thing?

SADIE. *Death is PURE sensation, didn't you know? I told you, this is very slightly radiated already.*

PEROWNE. By the Dutch people.

SADIE. *And me. It's only for the top meat, Perowne. Grade A Clears. Occupants of the 35th Bardo, and 7th Astral Plane. It's a Crux Ansata for hooking yourself out of samsara. Out of names and games. It's the biggest by-pass circuit of them all. Speed up your biological clock so that you can contract right out of time, and smash all those second hand pacemakers (Pointing to the wall of photos) smash all those electric pricks (Pointing to the TV) Clean up all your bad vibrations. Letting the spirits out of the hole, that was the Greek version of it. Thaumaturgic initiation into a higher caste.*

PEROWNE. (taking the trephine, and turning it over in his hands)
Block the openings, shut the doors, and all your life you won't
run dry. Unblock the openings, add to your troubles, and to
the end of your days you'll be beyond salva-tion. Lao Tzu.

SADIE. *Very nice, but there've been no trepanned skulls
ever found in China, as far as I know. Some of them
obviously had the Third Eye, but Lao Tzu can't ever
have got into it. Lotta creatures have it naturally.
The Sphenodon's got it. Ever had your hair punched
or popped? To spread out the follicles, if you're going
bald? Same scene with this. Scalp's got a very low
pain threshold. Osseous integuments got none.*

(SADIE sits PEROWNE down on the chair in front of
the table. She sits behind him on the table, massaging
his shoulders)

SADIE. *Got any cotton wool?*

(PEROWNE indicates a drawer. SADIE gets it and
stuffs some into PEROWNE's ears)

*So you can really get into it. Saw some pictures of the
Loyalty Islanders doing it with bits of broken glass,
and sharpened shells, and sharks teeth. It went on for
hours. You can really get into your head changes
when it goes on that long. They got male and female
trephines now, you know. Male one's got a spike in
the middle to position it right. This one's AC/DC.
(Pitching her voice low and rhythmical) Drive your
influencing machine on a completely different fuel.
Fire cells you haven't yet invested in. Wipe all your
information channels clean. It's gonna return you to
state zero an give you a double run. (She splashes the
bottle on Perowne's head) Those adrenal circuits.
Starve it to death. Auto-Rhythmical Mental Ice. Graft
new circuit space onto the neo-cortex. It hasn't been
there long, you gotta give it breathing room. Speed up
your mitochondria. Increase your channel capacity.
Speed up all your mutative patterns. You're gonna*

have a Real Fuckin Fuel Cell. (She holds the trephine above the left parietal zone) Are you prepared for this now? Good deeds can often be very shocking.

PEROWNE. I think so.

(SADIE clears his hair, and presses the trephine onto the scalp)

SADIE. *There really was a Lost Paradise dig? When the Deva Eye, the eye of Shiva was open, in the days of the Cyclopean root race . . . and then man fell into matter, and the Third Eye atrophied, leaving just the pineal gland as witness. A Lost Paradise of Lost Brain Blood Volume. Lost again when your fissures and fontanelles closed up at three. Lost again when your cranial sutures ossified. Lost when you stood vertical. More and more horrible adrenalin, the more upright you stood.*

(SADIE alternately pronates and supinates the trephine with her hand in neutral position)

Lost the brain as a valve. Lost the cerebral heart beat. Starved the neurones. Lost the cerebral pulsations. Starved the glia. Constricted the arterioles.

(Pressing the trephine down harder into PEROWNE's head)

So? Gotta correct the mechanism. Bring yourself back into the galactic metabolism. Let in some Light. Restore the Outside Pressure. Let in more Blood, and drive out that superfluous spoonful of cerebro-spinal fluid that's bringing you down . . .Can You Feel It? (Leaning over him) Can you feel it? It's comin out now, like a little slug of scum. Little spurt. Speut! It's warm.

(She lifts the trephine up, then replaces the trephine in the groove in PEROWNE's scalp, and continues

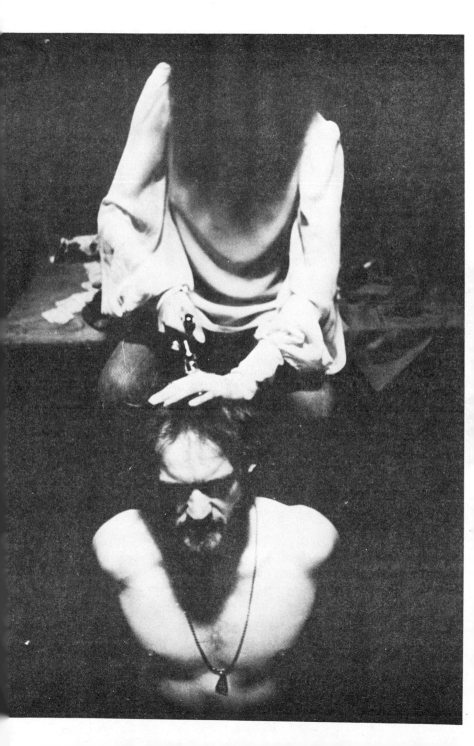

revolving)

Kundalini flame vibrations moving up and down your spine, opening all the chakras, burning out all the dross. Waiting until your brain is prepared for it to enter . . .

PEROWNE. I can feel no pain.

SADIE. *No, and soon that ego trip of YOU feeling pain, you thinking about you feeling pain, that'll disappear. It's a mind-body chakra to get the pineal gland pickin up on cosmic energy of the highest quality . . .*

PEROWNE. Suppose it doesn't work?

SADIE. *Suppose it doesn't? What were you doing with Maurice? Widening the irrational threshold right? Publicising the unofficial environment right? Giving the shadows genitals. So that some bureaucrat like me could come along, clean up on that energy, get it together and get us off the fuckin planet. (Pointing at the trephine in PEROWNE's head) Well this is the form you gotta fill in. We're gonna drop this planet like a hot potato.*

PEROWNE. Maurice kept talking about hollowing out.

SADIE. *Yeah. There's your synchronicity. He was pickin up paracognitive traces from the trephine in my suitcase.*

PEROWNE. I can feel the pressure changing. It's built up. It's a strange density. It doesn't hurt.

(SADIE removes the instrument, she pulls out the hair, scalp tissue and a small disc of bone from the teeth of the trephine. She stares down at PEROWNE)

SADIE. *It's the Total ESP Fuck. Eight orifices in your head now, Perowne. Get you responding to undiscovered electro-magnetic fields. Your psi-plasma field's now been uncoupled from gravitational contraction and adrenalin constipation. Whole of the Aztec Space People's civilisation was a trepanned society, Perowne. All had to have it done when they got here because the gravity wasn't right. They all had to decompress each other to keep in touch with the central morphogenetic psi-plasma field they'd left behind.*

(PEROWNE seems to be cutting off. SADIE scrutinises PEROWNE. He sits quite still. SADIE swabs his Third Eye)

(SILENCE)

I can feel you picking it up. There's a taste of the true heat around. Shit awful field flux. But there's some winner beams tryin to make it. Can you get a fix on their pitch?

(PEROWNE nods)

They're shifting all the spectral lines. They're shifting my detectability threshold. Gotta metabolise their radiations. It'll be like a couple of micro-cocaine flashes all over your astral tastebuds... VIBIN YOUR ASTRAL BODY, when they hit you. Stick out your psionic telescope. FURTHER. FURTHER.

PEROWNE. Above the ... above the ...

SADIE. *Yeah, like that. They'll get it. They'll get it. They're probably using some of Maurice's ectohormonal beams to track us.*

PEROWNE. Above the ... above the ...

SADIE. *That's all right. That's all right. They always get you into some bag like that when they first issue visas. Don't worry about that.*

(PEROWNE makes a series of small, non-cognitive movements)

SADIE. *FUUUUUUUUUUUUUUK! IT'S ON! Keep your mind still. They'll zap it in. They'll zap it in. Keep your mind still. FUUUUUCK! THEY'RE TWANGING THE WHOLE FUCKIN ELECTROMAGNETIC SPECTRUM. FUCKIN ANTI-MATTER TELEPATHONS FRIZZIN ME UP! OPEN YOUR CUNT TO THE SUN, PEROWNE, OPEN YOUR CUNT TO THE SUN!*

(PEROWNE makes a series of minute movements. SADIE holds her ears, then moves her hands through her hair, then squeezes her head)

Fuuck, they're Really shifting the field. 'Fuckin fifty seven thousand gauss. What is it? What is it? They're gettin us through to some Total Aggregate of Mental Fluid. CAN YOU FEEL THEM ENJOYING YOU?

(PEROWNE moves his limbs as if in low gravity. As SADIE speaks the resonance of her voice is totally altered as if the balance of the gases in the air has been altered. All cognitive clues as to their behaviour beginning to implode)

SADIE. *YOU'RE SO CLEAN NOW, PEROWNE. THEY'RE WHISTLING THROUGH YOU! (Snapping her fingers) I fucked it up calling you, Perowne. They don't use those shop soiled co-ordinate points. It's gettin attenuated again. Don't filter them. Little automatic gain control to boost it. (She tightens up her body. Giant breaths) Flashover the flashpoints of neuronic discharge to fetch them back... RADIATIVE COLLISION! FUCCK THEY'RE ONTO YOU! DON'T FILTER IT. DON'T FILTER IT. Bit of... I gotta Blip then... bit of magnetic torque... They're exploding psi-plasma blanks in my head, to black me out... to cut me out of the circuit to give you full*

*power. No, no they're not. DON'T FILTER THE
PULSES, PEROWNE... Full field. FULL FIELD.
Shit, did you feel that bit that went through then?
That was shorthand for a fuckin microcosm. That was
a Joke! Did you feel it?*

(PEROWNE nods; He stares at her and smiles)

SADIE. *They gotta socket now, you dig. They gotta Free
Connection Point. (She touches the hole in
PEROWNE's head) Don't flash out. Lay it all out
now. LAY IT OUT. All the the deepest coagulations.*

(PEROWNE makes a series of minimal facial expressions, corresponding to no known emotions)

SADIE. *Lay it out now... It's good... It's good. It's
... (She moves rapidly from side to side, emitting
high frequency clicking speech) It's trying to get
into... It's inter... kinetic... inter demalio... deliv-
ing... derrrthusp... derrthusp... derammm yeah
... delidio... decram... decramm... Feeling good
with it, yeah, it's... Pick it up again, Perowne. IT'S
FADING, PEROWNE. THE FUCKIN BUZZ IS
GOING OFF. PICK IT UP AGAIN, PEROWNE. STOP
CHANGING THE RATES. STOP CHANGING THE
RATES! They're preparing to do a real number on us
Play that fuckin E.S.P. riff you had going at the start
off... Play that again.*

PEROWNE. Above the... above the... Above the... (Metro-
nomic) I Like It Very Much.

SADIE. *Are you back into it? I can't feel it (She moves
her hands all over her body) I can't feel it. (She moves
off the table, and crouches over him) Gotto amplify
those fuckin vibes, man. Gotta draw ALL the vibes
down here. I don't think they're scrambling them.
Gotta get back through to it. There's a huge fuckin
vibesurge there floating round. It's fading... gotta...
(She puts her hand inside PEROWNE's fly) Bit of ESP*

Protein. Sharpen the impulses with a bit of sex static. Use it as an astral dowsing wand. Biolectric aerial to vampup the charge. They'll come back in now. Don't move the blood into your cock. Your brain's got an erection. That's why it's like that.

(PEROWNE stares down)

Hold that sex static just like it is. That's a heavy duty field they can find. Don't blow it. ARE YOU GETTING INTO IT AGAIN?

(PEROWNE nods. SADIE moves her hand inside his fly)

ARE YOU GETTING INTO IT AGAIN?

(PEROWNE closes his eyes)

SADIE. *OPEN YOUR EYES. Don't need any introspective freakshow to pick up these radiations. OPEN YOUR EYES. DON'T FLASH OUT ON ME. ARE YOU TRYING TO SCUTTLE THAT FUCKIN BUZZ? (She rubs his cock faster and faster) PICK IT UP, PICK IT UP. YEEEEEEEEEEEEEEAAAAAAAAAAAAAH! WHAT? WHAAAAAAAT? WHAAA Wow . . . wow . . .*

(SADIE tenses up, then discharges all her muscles. She flashes and creases, and stares. There is the sound of giant electronic breathing. The psychic static amplified. She claws at PEROWNE's body. Turning every cell of his body into a brain cell)

SADIE. *FUCKIN PARA-PIERCING VIBESURGE . . .*

THEY'RE FUCKIN YOU IN YOUR THIRD EYE NOW PEROWNE . . .

I MEAN THE STIFFEST E.S.P. RIFF EVER BLOWN!

DOUBLE EUPHORIA HEAD!

PLAY IT . . . PLAY IT . . . RELAY IT . . . RELAY IT!

GET INTO THEIR ASSEMBLY LANGUAGE. LAY IT OUT FOR ME! YOU GOT IT

YOU'RE HITTING IT . . . YOU'RE HITTING IT!

GET INTO THEIR ASSEMBLY LANGUAGE!

LAY IT OUT FOR ME

(PEROWNE opens his eyes slowly, raises his head, screams, and then turns and looks around, smiling)

PEROWNE.

C AND B PLAYSCRIPTS

		Cloth	Paper
*PS 1	TOM PAINE Paul Foster	£1.05	45p
*PS 2	BALLS and other plays (The Recluse, Hurrah for the Bridge, The Hessian Corporal) Paul Foster	£1.25	50p
PS 3	THREE PLAYS (Lunchtime Concert, The Inhabitants, Coda) Olwen Wymark	£1.05	35p
*PS 4	CLEARWAY Vivienne C. Welburn	£1.05	35p
*PS 5	JOHNNY SO LONG and THE DRAG Vivienne C. Welburn	£1.25	45p
*PS 6	SAINT HONEY Paul Ritchie	£1.25	55p
PS 7	WHY BOURNEMOUTH? and other plays (An Apple A Day, The Missing Link) John Antrobus	£1.25	50p
*PS 8	THE CARD INDEX and other plays (Gone Out, The Interrupted Act) Tadeusz Rozewicz tr. Adam Czerniawski	£1.25	55p
PS 9	US Peter Brook and others	£2.10	£1.25
*PS 10	SILENCE and THE LIE Nathalie Sarraute tr. Maria Jolas	£1.25	45p

		Cloth	Paper
*PS 11	THE WITNESSES and other plays (The Old Woman Broods, The Funny Old Man) Tadeusz Rozewicz tr. Adam Czerniawski	£1.50	60p
*PS 12	THE CENCI Antonin Artaud tr. Simon Watson Taylor	90p	40p
*PS 13	PRINCESS IVONA Witold Gombrowicz tr. Krystyna Griffith-Jones and Catherine Robins	£1.05	45p
*PS 14	WIND IN THE BRANCHES OF THE SASSAFRAS Rene de Obaldia tr. Joseph Foster	£1.25	45p
*PS 15	INSIDE OUT and other plays (Still Fires, Rolley's Grave) Jan Quackenbush	£1.05	45p
*PS 16	THE SWALLOWS Roland Dubillard tr. Barbara Wright	£1.25	55p
PS 17	THE DUST OF SUNS Raymond Roussel	£1.50	60p
PS 18	EARLY MORNING Edward Bond	£1.25	55p
PS 19	THE HYPOCRITE Robert McLellan	£1.25	50p
PS 20	THE BALACHITES and THE STRANGE CASE OF MARTIN RICHTER Stanley Eveling	£1.50	60p

		Cloth	Paper
*PS 31	STRINDBERG Colin Wilson	£1.05	45p
*PS 32	THE FOUR LITTLE GIRLS Pablo Picasso tr. Roland Penrose	£1.25	50p
PS 33	MACRUNE'S GUEVARA John Spurling	£1.25	45p
*PS 34	THE MARRIAGE Witold Gombrowicz tr. Louis Iribarne	£1.75	75p
*PS 35	BLACK OPERA and THE GIRL WHO BARKS LIKE A DOG Gabriel Cousin tr. Irving F. Lycett	£1.50	75p
*PS 36	SAWNEY BEAN Robert Nye and Bill Watson	£1.25	50p
PS 37	COME AND BE KILLED and DEAR JANET ROSENBERG, DEAR MR. KOONING Stanley Eveling	£1.75	75p
PS 38	DISCOURSE ON VIETNAM Peter Weiss tr. Geoffrey Skelton	£1.90	90p
*PS 39	! HEIMSKRINGLA ! or THE STONED ANGELS Paul Foster	£1.50	60p
*PS 41	THE HOUSE OF BONES Roland Dubillard tr. Barbara Wright	£1.75	75p
*PS 42	THE TREADWHEEL and COIL WITHOUT DREAMS Vivienne C. Welburn	£1.75	75p

		Cloth	Paper
PS 54	LONG VOYAGE OUT OF WAR Ian Curteis	£2.25	£1.05
PS 55	INUIT and THE OTHERS David Mowat	£1.75	75p
PS 57	CURTAINS Tom Mallin	£1.60	70p
PS 58	VAGINA REX AND THE GAS OVEN Jane Arden	£1.25	55p
*PS 59	SLAUGHTER NIGHT and other plays Roger Howard	£1.50	60p
PS 60	AS TIME GOES BY and BLACK PIECES Mustapha Matura	£2.25	£1.00
PS 61	MISTER and OH STARLINGS! Stanley Eveling	£1.75	75p
PS 62	OCCUPATIONS and THE BIG HOUSE Trevor Griffiths	£2.00	£1.00
*PS 64	MR. JOYCE IS LEAVING PARIS Tom Gallacher	£1.80	90p
PS 65	IN THE HEART OF THE BRITISH MUSEUM John Spurling	£2.00	£1.00
PS 66	LAY BY Howard Brenton and others	£1.80	90p

*All plays marked thus are represented for dramatic
presentation by:
C and B (Theatre) Ltd, 18 Brewer Street, London W1